'Having explored both the world of science and that of spirituality, I always appreciate books that strive to bring together these two great streams of human thought. Chaitanya Charan's *Demystifying Reincarnation* is one such book. The subject of reincarnation is indeed a mystery, because we can't know what happens after death. Or can we? Scientific studies of near-death experiences and past life memories, as analyzed in this book, point persuasively towards a part of us that survives death. Readers will be surprised to know that this inference has been reiterated by many of the world's most prominent thinkers throughout history. Chaitanya Charan's demystification of reincarnation by drawing from the wisdom texts of ancient India such as the Bhagavad Gita and the Upanishads is indeed intriguing and illuminating. Overall, *Demystifying Reincarnation* is an intellectually stimulating and spiritually uplifting book that will expand the readers' conceptions of life and its meaning.'

–Padma Vibhushan Dr. Vijay Bhatkar,
Chancellor, Nalanda University

'This may well be a major breakthrough work on reincarnation, and related subjects. Chaitanya Charan is known among writers and practitioners of Krishna-bhakti for his clear exposition, thorough analysis, and readable prose—this work is no exception. *Demystifying Reincarnation*, carefully studied, renders the mystery useless, like a snake without its teeth, and offers readers resolution for a problem long considered. I applaud Chaitanya Charan for this accessible and much-valued explanation of a dodgy subject. Well worth reading, even for those already well-versed in the existing literature on reincarnation.'

–Steven J. Rosen, author of *The Reincarnation Controversy*
and thirty books on spiritual topics, and founding
editor of the *Journal of Vaishnava Studies*

'The topic of reincarnation is indeed intriguing; are we actually eternal and beyond death? In this well-researched book, Chaitanya Charan addresses this topic from a variety of points of view. He offers evidence from scientific researchers, cites ancient wisdom texts as well as offers a historical survey of reincarnation in the classical traditions. He has written a fascinating book, which is not only historical or philosophical but spiritual as well, and is no doubt successful in demystifying this existential and complex issue. I found this book truly illuminating.'

–Dr. Ithamar Theodor, author of *Exploring the Bhagavad Gita; Philosophy, Structure and Meaning*

'Just as the discovery of something new is delightful, so is the rediscovery of the validity of something we have known. *Demystifying Reincarnation* offers such delightful confirmation of our gut feeling that we are meant for more than casual destruction at death. Those familiar with reincarnation will be enlivened to see such an array of evidence and reasoning marshalled in the service of this time-honoured concept. And those new to it will find in this soundly-reasoned book an irresistible invitation to the spiritual life they have been missing. Chaitanya Charan has rendered an invaluable service by authoring this insight-packed book about our core identity and ultimate destiny.'

–Hrishikesh Mafatlal, Chairman, Arvind Mafatlal Group

'I was convinced about the reality of reincarnation after having dealt with two of my pediatric patients who had elaborate memories of their past lives. I was looking for a scientific book on this subject, and Chaitanya Charan's *Demystifying Reincarnation* fulfills that need very scientifically and with a critical eye. More such studies are required to make reincarnation acceptable in today's world.'

–Dr. A. P. Sankhe, International President for Global Foundation for Ethics and Spiritual Health (GFESH); Director, Bhaktivedanta Hospital, Mumbai

Reprint 2020

FiNGERPRINT! BELIEF

An imprint of Prakash Books India Pvt. Ltd.

113/A, Darya Ganj, New Delhi-110 002,
Tel: (011) 2324 7062 – 65, Fax: (011) 2324 6975
Email: info@prakashbooks.com/sales@prakashbooks.com

facebook www.facebook.com/fingerprintpublishing
twitter www.twitter.com/FingerprintP, www.fingerprintpublishing.com

ISBN: 978 81 7599 433 1

Processed & printed in India

Dedicated to

MY MANY SPIRITUAL MENTORS,
Who have expanded my conception of life

&

MY MANY FRIENDS,
Whose questions inspire me to keep seeking
better understanding of life's timeless truths

CONTENTS

INTRODUCTION—A TELESCOPE TO SEE THE WORLD WITHIN

Since my childhood, I have been fascinated by science and its potential to uncover the truths of life in a logical and verifiable manner. I remember spending hours at night looking up at the vast sky through my telescope, wondering at the mysteries that the sky held and marvelling at the magical way the telescope made the distant close, the hazy clear, and the invisible visible.

Over the years, I found myself wondering whether there existed a telescope that I could turn on myself to look within for understanding who I actually was and the purpose of my existence.

In my youth, while pursuing my engineering studies, I discovered that telescope in the wisdom of the *Bhagavad-gita*. I found its teachings of yoga enormously empowering for myself and for those with whom I shared them; empowering in providing coherent answers and in effecting self-improvement.

Yet, the *Gita* telescope left me uncomfortable, for it was not the kind I had been looking for—it was metaphysical, not physical. At that time, I was apprehensive whether I would have to choose between science and spirituality. But surprisingly and thankfully, in my studies, I found that a significant body of scientific research supported many of the *Gita*'s fundamental tenets. The most important among such areas of the intersection of science and spirituality is consciousness and its possible origin in a non-material source like the soul, which, in turn, leads to the possibility of reincarnation.

As I studied both science and spirituality for over a decade and a half, I pored over scores of books that offered arguments and evidences supporting reincarnation. However, I realised that a book that systematically and coherently integrated all those around a reincarnation-centred worldview was acutely missing. This book is my attempt to fill that gap.

To help orient your reading of the book, here is a brief overview of its contents.

1. **Past-life Memories—1**

   The chapter starts with hypnotically induced past-life memories, highlighting cases in which the subjects exhibit xenoglossy, the ability to speak and write in foreign languages—especially languages that have been extinct for centuries. Then, it focuses on spontaneous past-life memories among children, using specific cases to evaluate whether the children's normal knowledge might have given rise to their past-life memories.

2. **Past-life Memories—2**

   The chapter explores more cases of past-life memories, investigating whether they are a result of the children's imagination, or their parents' exaggeration. The imagination hypothesis is challenged by the extent of detail and accuracy in the children's memories. The exaggeration hypothesis is challenged by the existence of written records of those memories, the occurrence of birthmarks that correlate with past-life wounds, and the presence of neutral third parties during the meeting between the children's present-life and past-life families.

3. **Past-life Memories—3**

The chapter investigates the possibility that the past-life memories may have originated in fraud, by either the parents or the investigators. The parental fraud hypothesis is questioned by the absence of any religious, financial, or reputational incentive for the parents in attempting a fraud, the difficulty in executing a fraud involving many people and, perhaps most significantly, by cases in which the children's memories and behaviours distress their parents. The investigator fraud hypothesis is questioned by the similarity in the pattern of past-life memories all over the world and the researchers' objective, methodical, and rigorous documentation of their findings.

4. **Near-death Experiences (NDEs)**

Many people who have had NDEs report empirically accurate perceptions during their NDEs. Through the careful, critical study of various cases, this chapter evaluates whether these perceptions can be accounted for by various normal explanations such as hallucinations, educated guesses, partial consciousness, and fraud.

5. **Who am I?**
   The chapter starts with five intuitive reflections about our identity and then examines the idea that the brain produces consciousness. It shows the inadequacies of this idea through several convergent areas of research such as the continuity of our memories despite the continuous regeneration of brain cells and the capacity of some people to function normally despite having nearly zero brain matter.

6. **Reincarnation in World History**
   Countering the common notion that reincarnation is an Eastern belief, the chapter shows that people in all the inhabited continents of the world have believed in reincarnation. This chapter challenges the notion that reincarnation is a New Age fad and shows that reincarnation has enjoyed acceptability and even respectability among thinkers who have pondered life's deepest questions throughout the ages, from the time of the Greek civilization and earlier.

7. **Soul-Searching—The Vedic Way**
   The last two chapters of the book focus on the Vedic texts of ancient India, which give the most extensive explanation of reincarnation. Drawing insights from these texts and especially the *Bhagavad-Gita*, this chapter outlines a model of the soul as an ontological, non-metaphorical entity. A diagrammatic presentation based on this model explains the features of near-death experiences and past-life memories that are unexplainable by conventional science.

8. **Reincarnations—The Hows and the Whys**

This chapter explains the mechanism of reincarnation and analyses the factors that determine the trajectory of our post-mortem journey. It also addresses various common questions about reincarnation such as: Do animals have souls? Can humans reincarnate as animals? Why can't we remember our past lives? How do we learn if we can't remember our past lives? Does genetics disprove reincarnation? and Does population explosion disprove reincarnation?

9. **Freedoms of the Reincarnation Worldview**

Understanding life with the help of a reincarnation-based worldview helps us make sense of the world's glaring inequities. It also empowers us to pursue our enlightened self-interest, thereby helping us realise our dormant spiritual potential. This worldview also brings significant freedom from humanitarian, economic, and ecological perspectives.

Appendix

1. **The Comeback of the Soul**

Since the time of Descartes, the problem of mind-matter interaction has seemed intractable, and has led to the exile of the soul from mainstream intellectual discourse. However, insights from the Vedic model, when combined with the implications of quantum physics, enable the soul to stage a comeback.

2. **Conscious Machines?**

Technological advances enable machines to replicate and even supersede the information processing capacities of consciousness. But those very advances also expose the yawning conceptual chasms that prevent machines from becoming conscious and also problematise all materialist attempts to explain consciousness.

3. **Ghosts Demystified**

The Vedic model of the self explains many other phenomena that, though widely documented, elude explanation by the conventional model of the self. To illustrate this explanatory versatility of the model, we consider one such phenomenon: the existence of disembodied beings. The Vedic model removes ghosts from the realm of the eerie, and brings them into the jurisdiction of the explainable. A diagrammatic analysis elucidates what ghosts are, who become ghosts, and why.

SETTING THE SCENE

❧

*"... Were an Asiatic to ask me for a definition of
Europe, I should be forced to answer him: it is that part
of the world which is haunted by the incredible delusion that
man was created out of nothing, and that his present
birth is his first entrance into life."*
–Arthur Schopenhauer, *Parerga and Paralipomena*, II

Reincarnation—the idea that we return in another body after the death of our current body—has fascinated people throughout history. All over the world, many cultures, ancient and modern, have included reincarnation as an integral part of their worldviews. Even Pharaonic Egypt, polytheistic Greece and Rome, Taoism, Zoroastrianism, and a large variety of shaman and tribal groups shared a common belief in reincarnation even when they had widely differing other beliefs. In the light of this overwhelming acceptance of reincarnation, Schopenhauer rightly considered the European disbelief in reincarnation an "incredible delusion."

With the global expansion of European colonialism, disbelief in reincarnation became widespread all over the world.

Nevertheless, even today, one-thirds of the world population believes in reincarnation. And interestingly, even in the sceptical West, a significant number of eminent figures have always accepted reincarnation. Here are a few of them:

- Pythagoras (Greek philosopher-mathematician circa 580 – 500 BC)
- Plato (Greek philosopher, 428 – 347 BC)
- Giordano Bruno (Italian philosopher, 1548 – 1600)
- François Voltaire (French philosopher, 1694 – 1778)
- Benjamin Franklin (US statesman, philosopher, and inventor, 1706 – 1790)
- John Adams (US president, 1735 – 1826)
- Johann Wolfgang von Goethe (German poet and dramatist, 1749 – 1832)
- William Wordsworth (English poet, 1770 – 1850)
- Ralph Waldo Emerson (US philosopher and writer, 1803 – 1882)
- Robert Browning (English poet, 1812 – 889)
- Richard Wagner (German composer, 1813 – 1883)
- Henry David Thoreau (US social critic, writer, and philosopher, 1817 – 1862)
- Walt Whitman (US poet, 1819 – 1892)
- Leo Tolstoy (Russian novelist and social critic, 1828 – 1910)
- Mark Twain (US writer, 1835 – 1910)
- George Bernard Shaw (British writer, 1856 – 1950)
- Henry Ford (US automobile pioneer, 1863 – 1947)
- Rudyard Kipling (English writer, 1865 – 1936)

- W. Somerset Maugham (English writer, 1874 – 1965)
- Carl Jung (Swiss psychiatrist and psychologist, 1875 – 1961)
- Isaac Bashevis Singer (US novelist and short-story writer, 1904 – 1991)

In addition to these renowned thinkers, today, even ordinary people are increasingly accepting reincarnation. According to a 2009 survey conducted by the Pew Research Forum, nearly 24% Americans believe in reincarnation. Europe shows similar statistics. Times certainly seem to have changed since Schopenhauer's wry observation.

What may have caused this change?
Surprisingly, science has contributed significantly to the increasing appeal and acceptance of reincarnation, as these three areas of scientific studies strongly point out:

1. Past-life memories
2. Near-death experiences
3. The mystery of consciousness

In keeping with the scientific method that combines empirical observations and theoretical postulations, the first two items in the above-mentioned list focus more on empirical evidence, while the last one focuses more on conceptual analysis. In the next three chapters, we will examine past-life memories, considering whether various normal explanations can account for these cases. In chapter four, we will apply a similar critical approach to near death experiences. In chapter five, we will look at the mystery associated with consciousness.

CHAPTER ONE

PAST-LIFE MEMORIES—KNOWLEDGE FROM NORMAL SOURCES?

"Man will occasionally stumble over the truth, but [he]
usually manages to pick himself up, walk over
or around it, and carry on."
—*Winston S. Churchill*

Let's begin our study of past-life memories with a celebrity case where the celebrity is walking his talk.

A Multi-Million Dollar Truth— the Sheikh Who Was a Hindu King

Arab Sheikh Saud bin Muhammed al-Thani, cousin of the ruling emir of Qatar and one of the world's biggest art purchasers, believes that he is the reincarnation of the late Hindu Maharaja, Yeshwant Rao Holkar II of Indore, India, also known as YRH. For Al-Thani, this idea is no casual fancy; it is a serious multi-million-dollar truth.

The billionaire Al-Thani's past-life rendezvous began on seeing a portrait of Holkar painted by American artist Man Ray. Al-Thani, who was born five years after Holkar's death in 1961, was struck by the close resemblance between himself and Holkar—the same oblong face, the same broad forehead, the same sharp equine nose, and the same pencil moustache. The striking similarities triggered a flood of memories that eventually convinced Al-Thani that he was Holkar, reincarnated.

Holkar, who had been a ruler based in Indore, had led a luxurious lifestyle. He had sponsored an entire cricket team for over two decades, and owned a fleet of vehicles, including six Bentleys and two airplanes. Al-Thani too has lived lavishly, but his lavishness is now directed towards collecting heirlooms from his previous life. He purchases almost everything linked to Holkar, from international art auctions and antique shops, whatever be the cost.

The Sheikh even visited Indore to collect everything related to the Holkars. Upena Bapna, great grandson of former prime minister of Indore, Siremal Bapna, told the Indian newspaper DNA, "A few years ago, several antique dealers tried to get in touch with me to solicit my help in procuring antiques and articles that had anything to do with YRH. It was then that I came to know that they were buying on behalf of the Sheikh, who fancied himself to be the reincarnation of the former ruler."

Indore-based historian and art dealer, Rajendra Singh, added, "Al-Thani has spent millions of dollars on antiques related to the Holkars—vintage photography, rare jewels, cars, textiles, Art Deco furniture—building up an entire YRH collection." Reputed to have unlimited funds, the Sheikh's motto while conquering art auctions is "whatever it takes." At times, he buys the entire collection on display, even if it costs far more than the estimated price.

In March 2011, at Christie's Paris auction, he bought the objects that German designer Eckart Muthesius had created for YRH. The Sheikh purchased a bookshelf, and pair of wall-mounted lamps crafted for the Indore royals for a whopping $1.5 million.

Al-Thani doesn't just surround himself with Holkar's things; he also poses as the late ruler for elaborate and expensive photo sessions. He has even modelled his Al Wahab estate in Doha on Manikbagh, YRH's official residence in Indore.

Al-Thani's belief in reincarnation is remarkable, not just because of the sheer amount of money he is spending on it but also because he is walking his talk in a culture that is not just apathetic, but often antipathetic, to belief in reincarnation.

Whenever such anecdotal accounts of past-life memories come up, a question that always hovers in the background is, you mean this is for real?

Many scientific researchers have taken this question seriously and have subjected the claims of past-life memories to rigorous scientific scrutiny. Past-life memories can be:

1. Hypnotically-induced, wherein the subject recollects the memories during hypnotic regression or
2. Spontaneous, wherein the subject recollects the memories without any intentional stimulation from anyone.

HYPNOTICALLY-INDUCED PAST-LIFE MEMORIES

During such memories, a willing subject is hypnotised, and then gently led backward into time by a series of questions. On being thus regressed, the subject often recollects memories of past lives, memories that are frequently accompanied with intense emotions.

Among the researchers who have investigated such hypnotically-induced past-life memories, perhaps the best-known is Brian Weiss, an Ivy League psychiatrist with degrees from Columbia University and Yale Medical School. He has reported in several of his books, including the best seller *Many Lives Many Masters*, that regression into past lives has helped cure many subjects of long-standing phobias and other psychological problems. A typical case may involve a patient with hydrophobia, who recollects drowning in a previous life during the regression and becomes free from the phobia after the regression.

However, other researchers have rightly pointed out that just because the recollections heal doesn't prove that they were real. The claimed past-life memories may well be just the imagination of the subject, triggered by the questions of the therapist, and the subject's prior belief in, or receptivity to belief in reincarnation. These cautious researchers have argued that even if a subject gives verifiable information about a remote past-life, such information might be derived from the subject's prior general knowledge of history. For many cases, this is certainly possible and even probable. But in some significant cases, especially those involving xenoglossy, this seems improbable, if not impossible. Let's look at such cases.

A Case of Xenoglossy in an Extinct Language

The term xenoglossy was coined by Nobel Laureate French physiologist. Charles Richet (1850 – 1935) and is derived from the Greek prefix xeno, meaning "strange" or "foreign," and the word glossa, meaning "tongue." Xenoglossy, then, refers to the ability to speak or write in a language that could not have been acquired by normal, natural means.

Joel Whitton, a professor of psychiatry at the University of Toronto Medical School, reports a case of xenoglossy in his book *Life Between Life,* co-authored with best-selling author, Joe Fisher. A young American named Harold Jaworski recollected, during hypnotic regression, a past life as a Viking named Thor. When Whitton instructed him to write down, phonetically, the vocal exchanges he that he was recollected, he wrote down twenty-two words and phrases, none of which he himself understood on coming out of regression.

Whitton submitted the transcripts produced by Harold to several authorities in Icelandic and Norwegian languages. Working independently, they identified ten of those words as belonging to Old Norse, an extinct language spoken by the Vikings, primarily during 700-1300 CE. Several other words were identified as being of Russian, Serbian, or Slavic derivation. A majority of the words related to the sea, as would be natural for a seafaring community like the Vikings.

Thor Jakobsson, a research scientist with Canada's Department of the Environment, and an expert on the Icelandic language, observed that some of the words originated in other languages. This observation only added to the authenticity of the script, because such verbal eclecticism was to be expected in the language of the restless, warlike Vikings who roamed to the far corners of Europe.

During another regression session, Harold recollected another past life as a Mesopotamian named Xando. Whitton asked him to write down the words for common concepts, such as "brother," "house," and "clothing." Harold held a pencil very lightly and carefully created a mysterious, Arabic-style script in a spidery, childlike hand.

On coming out of hypnosis, Harold reported his own response to what he had just written: "When I looked at what I had done, all I could see was a bunch of squiggles . . . I thought it was pure garbage."

Whitton, however, felt that his writing merited careful investigation. He tried to find matches between Harold's mysterious pencil markings and ancient scripts in library books, but found none. Then, he submitted them to Ibrahim Pourhadi, an expert in ancient Persian and Iranian languages, at the Near Eastern Section of Washington's Library of Congress. After examining the samples closely, Pourhadi declared that they were an authentic representation of a long-extinct language named Sassanid Pahlavi. This language was used in Mesopotamia between 226 and 651 AD.

Eminent parapsychological investigators ranging from William James to Ian Stevenson have examined cases of xenoglossy. They have found numerous cases in which subjects, under hypnosis, communicate in a wide variety of foreign languages to which they had no exposure in their current life. These languages have ranged from modern European languages to ancient Chinese and even jungle dialects.

Among all these xenoglossy cases, Harold's case is distinctive, if not unique, as Whitton explains, "Harold is quite possibly the only human being to demonstrate the ability to communicate in two verifiable languages that no longer exist."

This distinctiveness of Harold's case is also its greatest strength. The languages he wrote in are no longer in use. In fact, Sassanid Pahlavi bears no resemblance to modern Iranian.

So, he could not have learnt those languages from anyone in the normal course of events. How, then, might he have learnt them? The only normal way to learn them today is to take long, specialised training under the few experts who know these languages. But Harold had never done such a thing, as was evident from his own inability during normal consciousness to even read, leave alone write in those languages. How, then, was he able to write in those languages during hypnosis? Might he have lived at the times when those languages were spoken, learnt them during those lives, and accessed that knowledge from his subconscious during the regression?

SPONTANEOUS PAST-LIFE MEMORIES

Let us now focus on past-life memories that are spontaneous, rather than hypnotically induced. As compared to hypnotically induced past-life memories, spontaneous past-life memories are more credible as these are not influenced by the hypnotists' suggestions or the subjects' increased suggestibility during hypnosis.

Thousands of cases involving spontaneous past-life memories have been investigated by researchers all over the world. The pioneer among these frontline researchers was the late Ian Stevenson, Carlson Professor of Psychiatry and Director of the Division of Personality Studies at the University of Virginia. Stevenson investigated the spontaneous past-life memories of more than three thousand children for over four decades and across five continents.

Let's begin by looking at one of the cases documented by Stevenson in his book *Reincarnation and Biology: A Contribution to the Etiology of Birthmarks and Birth Defects*.

The Case of the Pollock Twins

Gillian and Jennifer Pollock were two identical twins born in 1958 in Hexham, Northumberland, England. Their family moved away from Hexham when the twins were nine months old.

1. When they were about three, their mother overheard them talking repeatedly about their older sisters, Joanna and Jacqueline. Specifically, they mentioned details of the tragic accident that killed their sisters. While they had been walking to church, a crazed car driver had struck them fatally. This happened a year and a half before the twins were born.

2. Once, their parents unpacked two dolls belonging to their older daughters—dolls they had packed away after the girls' death. As soon as the twins saw those dolls, Gillian claimed the doll that had belonged to Joanna, the older of the two deceased sisters as her own while Jennifer claimed Jacqueline's. They added that Santa Claus had given them the dolls. The older sisters had received them as Christmas presents.

3. Gillian, on seeing a toy clothes wringer, a Christmas gift of Joanna's, promptly declared, "Look! There is my toy wringer." Again, she said that Santa Claus had given it to her.

4. One day, their father, while painting, wore a smock that their mother had previously used when the older girls were alive. When Jennifer saw the smock on her father, she asked him, "Why are you wearing Mummy's coat?" When he asked her how she knew that it was her

mother's coat, she answered correctly that her mother had worn it while breastfeeding her deceased daughters.

5. When the twins were four, the family made a day trip to Hexham, for the first time after the twins' birth. There, the family started walking along a road near a park where the older girls had often played, when the twins exclaimed that they longed to cross the road, enter the park, and play on the swings. Neither the swings nor even the park was visible from the road.

All these actions of the twins prompted their mother, who had not believed in reincarnation, to start believing that they were her older daughters, reincarnated.

This case is just one of the thousands that researchers have discovered and documented of children giving unusual, if not extraordinary information about a deceased person whom researchers call the "previous personality." How could these children have known about the previous personality? In fact, information is just one of the four intriguing features of such cases, features that beg for explanation. These features are:

1. **Recollections**: The children recollect many accurate details connected with the life of a deceased person, who they claim to have been in a past life.

2. **Recognitions**: When these children are taken to the place where the previous personality had lived, they often recognise people, places, and objects related to the previous personality.

3. **Birthmarks and birth defects**: Many of these children often have distinctive birthmarks or birth defects in the

same bodily locations where the previous personality had fatal wounds.

4. **Behaviours**: Some of these children often have phobias for activities and places associated with the previous personality's death. Some of them also exhibit philias (likings) for those activities that the previous personality liked.

How can these features be explained? Researchers have posited four broad explanations:

1. Information by normal means
2. Guesswork
3. Exaggeration
4. Fraud

We will evaluate each explanation individually in this, and the next two chapters.

Let's consider the first explanation.

FIRST NORMAL EXPLANATION: INFORMATION BY NORMAL MEANS

Could the children have heard about the previous life from a normal source and forgotten the source? Going back to the Pollock case, could the twins have learnt about their older sisters from their mother, but had forgotten about it? Could be. But this would explain only their memories of their deceased sisters, not their self-identification with them.

Moreover, this explanation can't clarify cases in which the previous personality had not been a family member. In most cases, the previous personality had lived a considerable distance away from the children's hometowns. The children's family or acquaintances had not known them. The previous personalities had led uneventful lives that had not been covered in any public media such as newspapers or television, accessible to the children. In fact, cases in which the previous personalities were complete strangers to the children and their families are far more common than the cases in which the previous personalities were relatives.

Let's look at one such case that was broadcast on the ABC television network.

Case with Information Too Obscure to Be Known: James Leininger

James, a boy born to educated American parents Andrea and Bruce Leininger, started having nightmares when he was two. He would scream in terror and would say, "Airplane crash, on fire, little man can't get out." Coincidentally, from his early childhood, he played primarily and often exclusively with planes and showed extraordinary knowledge of fighter planes, despite never having watched war documentaries. At three, he would inspect a toy plane systematically, as if he were doing a pre-flight checkup.

On one occasion, when Andrea pointed to what she thought was a bomb on the back of a toy plane, he corrected her, saying that it was a drop tank. Andrea had never heard of a drop tank till then. When she read about planes, she found that not only was James right, but that he knew more about planes than she did.

When James' nightmares increased in intensity and frequency, his parents took him to therapist-counsellor Carol Bowman, who had researched and written on past-life memories in children. Although James' parents didn't believe in reincarnation, they were ready to try out anything as long as it relieved their son of his nightmares.

During her counselling, Bowman encouraged them to let James speak about his nightmares. When they did so, to their pleasant surprise, his nightmares soon decreased and eventually disappeared. To their even greater surprise, he started revealing, before falling asleep at night extraordinary details about his past-life as a World War II fighter pilot killed by the Japanese. One by one, he revealed details which, on investigation, Bruce found to be true, but which would have been increasingly unlikely for an American boy to know. James mentioned the following details:

1. That he had flown a Corsair, and that those planes "used to get flat tires all the time." Bruce found that Corsairs did indeed have that defect.
2. That he had taken off from a boat named the Natoma and had flown off with a "Jack Larson." It turned out that the Natoma Bay was a small aircraft carrier in the Pacific. Also, Jack Larson, an ex-fighter pilot, was still alive and living in Arkansas.
3. That he was shot down at Iwo Jima, sustaining a direct hit on the engine. James also started signing his crayon drawings "James 3." Research showed that the only pilot from the Natoma's squadron killed at Iwo Jima was a James M. Huston Jr. The Jr. or "second" in that name explained why James, who thought of himself as the reincarnation, signed himself as James 3. Ralph Clarbour, a rear gunner on the plane flying right next

to James M. Huston Jr. during the Iwo Jima raid, confirmed little James' account of how the plane had been hit by anti-aircraft fire. "I would say he was hit head on, right in the middle of the engine."

The confluence of all this evidence chipped away Bruce's scepticism, fully convincing him that his son was indeed a reincarnation of James M. Huston Jr. Bruce. His wife further went on to describe their son's extraordinary experiences in a full book, *Soul Survivor: The Reincarnation of a World War II Fighter Pilot*.

For the purpose of our analysis, the key point is that James couldn't have acquired this remarkable information by normal means. Why not? Because the information was neither known nor readily accessible even to his parents, who had to do extensive research to confirm it.

Let's consider another case where a child had information that was too intimate to be normally known. This case is from Ian Stevenson's book *Twenty Cases Suggestive of Reincarnation*.

Case with information too intimate to be known: Shanti Devi

On 11 December 1926 Babu Rang Bahadur Mathur of Chirawala Mohulla, a small locality in Delhi, had a daughter and he named her Shanti Devi.

When she was four years old, she started talking about her "husband" and her "children." She referred to herself as a *Chaubine* (Chaube's wife), and mentioned three distinctive features about her husband: he was fair, had a big wart on his left cheek, and wore reading glasses. She also stated that her husband's shop was located in Mathura in front of the Dwarkadhish temple.

When she was six years old, she even gave a detailed account of her death, following childbirth. When their family physician heard this, he was amazed at how a little girl could describe the complicated surgical procedure in such detail.

Despite being repeatedly asked, she refused to mention her husband's name out of deference to the custom among wives in India of not uttering their husbands' name. Finally, when a relative Babu Bishanchand promised to take her to Mathura if she mentioned her husband's name, she whispered it in his ear: Pandit Kedarnath Chaube.

When Kedarnath heard about Shanti Devi's memories, he visited her with his family on 12 November 1935.

1. She correctly identified him as her husband, although he had been intentionally introduced as her husband's brother.

2. When Kedarnath was offered his favourite food items, stuffed potato *paranthas* (a type of fried pancake) and pumpkin squash, he was amazed—more so when informed that Shanti Devi had specifically told her mother to cook those items, as they were his favourites.

3. Shanti Devi became emotionally overwhelmed on seeing Naveen, her son from her past-life (who was now just slightly older than her), embraced him, shed tears of joy, and rushed to bring him toys to play with.

4. Pointing at Kedarnath's present wife, she asked him, "Why did you marry her? Had we not decided before

my death that you would not marry again?" Kedarnath was left speechless.

5. That night, Kedarnath asked her about her fatal pregnancy. She had been suffering from arthritis at the time and was unable to get up; how had she conceived? Shanti Devi described the full process of intercourse with him, leaving no doubt in his mind that she was the reincarnation of his former wife Lugdi Bai, who had died from post-delivery complications on 4 October 1926—one year, ten months, and seven days before the birth of Shanti Devi.

Her story spread all over the country and reached the ears of Mahatma Gandhi, who appointed a committee of fifteen people including reputed national leaders, eminent lawyers, and respected journalists to investigate the case. Prominent among the committee members were: N. R. Sharma, leader of the National Congress Party of India, and a close associate of Gandhi; Lala Deshbandhu Gupta, managing director of *Daily Tej*, the leading newspaper of Delhi; and T. C. Mathur, a leading attorney from Delhi.

These committee members took her to Mathura on 24 November 1935, and what transpired thereafter became history. Here are the salient points from the committee's written report:

6. When little Shanti reached the Mathura railway platform and was in L Deshbandhu's arms, she was asked whether she recognised an elderly man wearing typical Mathura attire who had arrived and mixed in the small crowd. She spontaneously got down from L

Deshbandhu's arms, reverently touched the stranger's feet, and stood aside. When asked, she whispered in L. Deshbandhu's ear that the person was her *"Jeth"* (her husband's older brother). Her identification was spot on; the man was Babu Ram Chaubey, who was Kedarnath's older brother.

7. When they boarded a *tonga* (horse-driven carriage), she effortlessly guided them to Kedarnath's house.

8. On reaching the house, she not only identified all the members correctly but also dealt with each of them in the way appropriate for a traditional Indian housewife, even evincing the apt emotions for each relationship.

9. She also showed accurate knowledge of details of the house, such as the location of the erstwhile well where she used to bathe and the place where she had hidden money.

10. Even more remarkable was her correct explanation of the meaning of the words *jajroo* (lavatory) and *katora* (a type of fried pancake, normally known in India as parantha) because these words are used only by the Chaubes of Mathura and are normally unknown to outsiders.

Overall, Stevenson noted that Shanti Devi made at least 24 statements of her memories that matched the verified facts.

When the Shanti Devi case gained international fame, Swedish critic and award-winning journalist Sture Lonnerstrand travelled to India with the explicit purpose of exposing it. However, when he examined the case systematically, he found the evidence so persuasive that he ended up writing a book explaining how and why the case was authentic: *I Have Lived Before: The True Story of the Reincarnation of Shanti Devi.*

For our analysis, the relevant point is that Shanti Devi just couldn't have known by any normal means the details of Lugdi's personal life, especially her intercourse with her husband.

Cases like those of James Leininger and Shanti Devi are some of the many cases that defy the explanation of information by normal means. If the children don't get the information about their claimed past lives by normal means, then how do they get it? Could it be guesswork? Might they be imagining the information, and getting it right by chance?

We will analyse this possibility in the next chapter.

TO SUMMARISE

In this chapter, we discussed one celebrity case of past-life memories and one case of xenoglossy during hypnotically-induced past-life memories. Then, we zeroed in on spontaneous past-life memories among children. After going over one introductory case, we noted the four principal features of such cases and the four possible normal explanations. While evaluating the explanation of information by normal means, we reviewed two cases in which the information was too specific or intimate to have been acquired by normal means.

In the next chapter, we will analyse the next two explanations: guesswork, and exaggeration.

CHAPTER TWO

PAST-LIFE MEMORIES—GUESSWORK OR EXAGGERATION?

"There are more things in heaven and earth, Horatio,
Than are dreamt of in your philosophy."
—Shakespeare, Hamlet, act 1, scene 5

In the previous chapter, we started the discussion on past-life memories to evaluate whether they offer any empirical pointers towards reincarnation. As the most credible pointers are likely to come from the cases of spontaneous past-life memories among children, we focused on cases of this genre. We also discussed how the first normal explanation—that the children acquired the information about the past-life by normal means—does not account for many of the cases.

In this chapter, we will evaluate the next two explanations: guesswork and exaggeration.

SECOND NORMAL EXPLANATION: INFORMATION BY GUESSWORK

The guesswork explanation holds that the children acquired whatever information they have about a past-life by guessing and getting it right by chance. This explanation is plausible in those cases where the children describe only generic details like the way of death in a past-life. However, in most of the cases, the children give information that is specific, detailed, and accurate.

Let's consider a case of this type.

Case with Information Too Specific to Be Guessed: Nazih Al-Danaf

Researcher Erlendur Haraldsson of the Department of Psychology, University of Iceland, Reykjavik, Iceland, investigated this Lebanese case with the assistance of Majd Abu-Izzeddin and published it in *The Journal of Scientific Exploration Vol 16, No 3*.

Nazih was born on 29 February 1992 in Baalchmay, Lebanon, as the eighth child of Sabir Al-Danaf and Naaim Al-Danaf. When Nazih was only a year and a half old, he started using words that his parents didn't expect a child of his age to know. He said that he carried two pistols and four hand-grenades and further stated that he was a fearless strong man, had a mute friend, a house with a cave close to it, and young children that he wanted to see. He also said that he had been shot by a group of men. He even told his mother and his six sisters, "My wife is prettier than you. Her eyes and mouth are more beautiful."

He repeatedly requested his parents to take him to Qaberchamoun, a small town about seventeen kilometres away and threatened to walk there by himself if they didn't take him. His parents, fearing that their son may go away forever, kept putting off his request for over four years.

When Nazih was six years old, his insistence finally forced his parents to drive him to Qaberchamoun. There, they came to a point where six roads converged. When Nazih's father asked him which way to go, he pointed to one of the roads. He said that they should drive in that direction until they reached a road that forked off upward, where they would see his house. When they reached the locality described by Nazih, they quickly discovered on enquiry that a person named Fuad Khaddage, who had owned a house there and had died ten years ago, matched Nazih's description. Here is what transpired next:

1. Nazih recognised as his wife Fuad's widow Najdiyah, who asked several questions to verify his claim.

2. Najdiyah asked, "Who built the foundation of this gate at the entrance of the house?"
   Nazih replied correctly, "A man from the Faraj family."

3. Najdiyah probed further, "Did I have any accident at our previous house?"
   Again, Nazih answered precisely, "Yes. One morning, while picking pinecones for our children to play, you skidded on plastic nylon, fell, and dislocated your shoulder."

4. Najdiyah asked, "Do you remember how our young daughter got seriously sick?"
   Yet again, Nazih was dead on. "She took my medication pills from my jacket and got poisoned by them. Then I took her to the hospital."

5. Najdiyah showed Nazih a photo of Fuad and asked him, "Who is this?" and Nazih replied immediately, "This is me; I was big, but now I am small."

Soon after this meeting with the family in Qaberchamoun, Nazih visited Fuad's younger brother Sheikh Adeeb at his home in Kfermatta.

6. As soon as Nazih saw Adeeb he announced to his family members, "Here comes my brother Adeeb." Then he ran over to Sheikh Adeeb and embraced him, saying, "I am your brother Fuad."

7. The surprised, somewhat sceptical Sheikh Adeeb asked, "What is the proof that you are Fuad?" Nazih reminded him, "I gave you a Checki 16." Fuad had indeed given such a gun to Adeeb.

8. After Nazih gave several correct pieces of information about Fuad, Sheikh Adeeb showed Nazih a photo with three persons in it. Nazih correctly identified each one of them as Adeeb, Fuad, and their third brother, Ibrahim.

9. When Sheikh Adeeb asked him where he had lived, Nazih led him out of the house and walked a short distance. Then, pointing to two adjacent houses he rightly identified his own house and his father's, too.

Let's look at the broad contours of this case.

Before Nazih was taken to Fuad's town, he had made seventeen statements corresponding correctly with the facts related to Fuad Khaddage's life. That he had actually made those statements was confirmed by not just one or two, but nine witnesses: his seven siblings and parents, all of whom gave consistent reports.

On reaching Fuad's place, he made at least eight additional

accurate statements about his former life, most of which were highly specific, like those about the Checki 16 and the man from the Faraj family. Moreover, he recognised seven persons, either on meeting them, or from their photos. In several of these recognitions, Nazih stated not just the relationship of the person with him but also the name of the person. For Sheikh Adeeb, the statement about the Checki 16 gun was decisively convincing. Why? Firstly, because Checki 16 is a gun from Czechoslovakia that is not common in Lebanon. And secondly, because nobody knew about the gun transaction except Fuad, Sheikh Adeeb, and possibly Adeeb's wife. Consequently, Nazih's knowledge of it convinced Adeeb that Nazih was Fuad reincarnated.

Just to crosscheck, Sheikh Adeeb visited Nazih later and showed him a gun different from the Checki 16 he had got from Fuad. When he asked, "Was this the gun you had given me?" Nazih answered promptly, "No."

For our analysis, the key point is the improbability of Nazih getting the many specific details right by chance. In Haraldsson's words: "We may ask how many of the men who died in the war had a mute friend and a cave near their house, had given their brother a Checki 16 pistol, and had a gate built in front of their house by a man from the Faraj family. In this case the combined odds against chance seem very high indeed."

Nazih's case is representative of the many cases in which the children give information that is too specific, detailed, and accurate to be accounted for by guesswork.

If the children's past-life memories cannot be explained as a result of guesswork, then how else can they be explained? Might they be products of exaggeration?

THIRD NORMAL EXPLANATION: EXAGGERATION

The exaggeration explanation holds that the case has been exaggerated by those involved—especially the child's relatives and the previous personality's relatives. Researchers have identified that such exaggeration is most likely to happen when the child meets the previous personality's family.

During that meeting, the previous personality's relatives may become overly excited at the prospect of a dead relative's return. So they may give the child unintentional cues, thus enabling him or her to identify more than what would have been normally possible. Or the relatives may unconsciously blow up the child's statements, crediting him or her with having identified more than the actual number of recognitions.

The best way to prevent such exaggeration is to have a past-life investigator intervene in the case before the crucial meeting between the child and the past-life relatives. The investigator can:

1. Make precise notes on the information the child gives before that meeting.
2. Arrange and oversee the meeting in such a way that nobody gives any cues to the child.
3. Ensure that the child's words and behaviour are objectively documented, say, through a tape recorder.

However, it's not easy for the investigators to intervene before the meeting. That's because cases occur in various parts of the world, including remote villages, and researchers come to know about a case only when it becomes well-known. And often, a case becomes well-known only after the child meets the previous personality's family and makes multiple correct recognitions.

Nonetheless, in a significant number of cases investigators, by their alertness and promptness have reached the case venue before the crucial meeting. In these cases, they have recorded the statements of the child before the meeting; ensured carefully monitored conditions for the meeting; and then observed, documented, and evaluated the statements and behaviour of the child during the meeting.

Let's look at one such case reported by Canadian researcher Antonia Mills, in *The Journal of Scientific Exploration*, Vol. 18, No. 4, pp. 609 – 641, 2004.

Case with Written Records Prior to Key Meeting: Ajendra Singh Chauhan

Ajendra, a boy born in northern India on 8 August 1978 was very aggressive from his early childhood.

1. When he was three, his aunt offered him a glass of milk. He responded by physically striking out at her in anger, shouting, "Two water buffaloes used to give milk. I used to drink a bucket of milk, and you brought this little."
2. Ajendra then said that his family had also owned a mare.
3. Sometime later, when Ajendra was still three, he was lying on his father's chest on the roof of their dwelling on a hot summer night. All of a sudden, he said, "Papa, the dacoits came. I started shooting from the raised wall at the edge of the roof and the bullet hit me."

4. Then Ajendra mimed crouching behind his father and shooting at the dacoits with a gun; he even mimed bending and straightening the gun to reload it. His behaviour was not just strange but remarkable, because at that tender age he had never seen dacoits and his father did not have a gun.

5. Despite his usually aggressive nature, he had a phobia of the dark that persisted until he turned thirteen. One night his father took his family to his natal village to celebrate Diwali. Ajendra urged his father to stop, saying, "Daddy, don't go to the garden in the dark. Dacoits live there. Sometimes police get killed, sometimes dacoits."

6. Subsequently, nudged by his father Ajendra gave many more details about his earlier life in a village named Fariha, some 75 kilometers from Ajendra's home.

Gaj Raj Singh Gaur, a junior college teacher and one of Stevenson's assistants, recorded Ajendra's case and found a deceased person named Naresh Chana Gupta in Fariha who matched Ajendra's description. On Gaur's invitation, Antonia Mills, a researcher at the University of Northern British Columbia, Canada, arrived to investigate the case. Mills crosschecked Gaur's written record of Ajendra's statements by interviewing him and his family once again. Then Mills and Gaur took Ajendra along with several of his family members to meet Naresh's family, which had frequently shuttled between their two houses—one in Fariha and one in Shekhanpur. Ajendra had mentioned many details about his past-life, some of which matched the house in Fariha and others, the house in Shekhanpur.

On enquiring with Naresh's family, Mills found that their family did indeed have two buffaloes and a mare at Shekhanpur, and Naresh had the habit of drinking unusually large quantities of milk. Moreover, Naresh had been shot and killed by dacoits while he had been trying to shoot at them with his gun from the roof of his house in Shekhanpur. The gun that he had been using during this fatal encounter was a Greener made in Birmingham. This gun, being bolted or cocked, needed to be bent out by pushing down on a shaft and then straightened again, just as Ajendra had mimed.

Altogether, as many as twenty-five of the details given by Ajendra turned out to be correct when applied to Naresh. Leading past-life researcher Bill Tucker has developed a Strength of Case Scale (SOCS) to evaluate the evidence of past-life memories cases. Mills analysed Ajendra's case using this scale and found it to be very strong: it was rated among the top three to five percent of all the cases among Tucker's samples.

For our analysis, the pertinent point is that in Ajendra's case the memories can't be explained away as exaggeration because his statements were noted down and crosschecked before the first meeting between the two families.

Let's now consider another case in which the possibility of exaggeration is almost entirely ruled out by the presence of a neutral third person and multiple observers at the time of the critical meeting when significant recognitions took place.

Case with Precise Recognitions under Multiple Supervision: Gnanatilleka

Gnanatilleka Baddewithana, who was born in Sri Lanka in 1956, began recollecting a past life from the age of two. She said that she had, in another place, a mother, father, two brothers, and many sisters. When Gnanatilleka heard about a town Talawakelle that was sixteen miles away, she started saying that she had lived there and that she wanted to go and meet her former parents there.

When she was four and a half years old, a neighbour wrote about her to a local journalist who had written several articles about reincarnation. The journalist H.S.S. Nissanka, who later earned a Ph.D. in International Relations, investigated the case systematically and went on to describe his findings in a book titled *The Girl Who Was Reborn: A Case-Study Suggestive Of Reincarnation.*

When Nissanka went to see Gnanatilleka, he took with him a well-known Buddhist monk and a teacher from a nearby college. When they interviewed Gnanatilleka, she described several incidents from a life in Talawakelle and talked about a sister whom she called Lora or sometimes, Dora.

Nissanka compiled the case details together in two articles that were published in a popular weekly newspaper. Subsequently the three men went to Talawakelle and on further investigation, found that Gnanatilleka's description matched that of a teenage boy named Tillekeratne who had died in November of 1954. To check the authenticity of this match, Nissanka planned a series of tests:

1. Three people from Talawakelle—Tillekeratne's teacher and two men who had been unknown to Tillekeratne—were asked to visit Gnanatilleka. When they asked her if she recognised them, she answered immediately in the negative for the last two men. To the teacher, she

first said that he was from Talawakelle and, after a moment's thought, added that he had taught her and had never punished her. Then she happily climbed into his lap.

2. The next day, the three-member investigation team took Gnanatilleka to a rest house in Talawakelle without telling her the reason for the trip, which was to arrange a meeting between her and Tillekeratne's family. The meeting was methodically set up with Gnanatilleka seated in a room with her mother, the monk, and Nissanka who had a tape recorder to record the events. Gnanatilleka's father and Tillekeratne's teacher stood at the door. Several observers watched from an adjacent room.

   i.   Tillekeratne's mother was told to enter the room. Pointing to her, the monk asked Gnanatilleka, "Do you know her?" As soon as Gnanatilleka looked at her, she suddenly appeared excited and continued gazing at her. On being asked for a second time whether she knew her, Gnanatilleka said, "Yes." Tillekeratne's mother gave Gnanatilleka a candy bar and held her arms out invitingly to the girl who promptly embraced her. When Tillekeratne's mother prompted Gnanatilleka, "Tell me, where did I live?" she slowly answered, "Talawakelle." Tillekeratne's mother then prodded her, "So tell me who I am." Gnanatilleka looked around to make sure that she was not within the hearing range of her own mother and then whispered to Tillekeratne's mother (and into Nissanka's microphone), "Talawakelle mother." After a minute's pause, the observers repeated the same question, "Who was that lady . . . tell us." This time, she replied in a normal voice, "She's my Talawakelle mother."

ii. Then, Tillekeratne's father was sent in and Gnanatilleka was asked, "Do you know him?" When she said yes, she was asked to identify him and she answered, "He's my Talawakelle father."

iii. Following him, one of Tillekeratne's sisters who used to accompany him to school every day, entered and Gnanatilleka was asked to identify her. She answered, "This is my sister from Talawakelle." When asked a further specific question, "Where did you go with this sister?" Gnanatilleka replied, "To school."

iv. Next came a man who had started living in Talawakelle after the death of Tillekeratne. When Gnanatilleka was asked repeatedly whether she knew him, she firmly gave the same answer, "No."

v. Subsequently, three other sisters of Gnanatilleka entered the room. When one of them asked Gnanatilleka, "Do you know me? Who am I?" she answered, "Yes, you're my fair sister." When the second woman asked her, "Who am I?" she answered, "The sister who lives in the house below ours." When Gnanatilleka's mother asked her who the third woman was, she responded with, "The sister to whose house we go to sew clothes." All the three answers were correct.

vi. After a few other identifications, the last person to enter was Tillekeratne's brother. He and Tillekeratne used to quarrel constantly. When Gnanatilleka was asked if she knew him she became angry and said, "No!" When she was asked the same question again she responded even more emotionally, "No! No!" Then Nissanka suggested that she could disclose only to her mother if she knew him. Gnanatilleka immediately whispered to her mother, "My brother from Talawakelle." Then Nissanka encouraged her to let everyone else hear and she said in her normal voice, "My brother from Talawakelle." When Nissanka requested Gnanatilleka to let the brother hold her, she began crying and replied that she would not.

3. Later, Gnanatilleka made two more spontaneous recognitions. As she had developed a relationship with Tillekeratne's teacher, she would go out with him. Once when they were out together Gnanatilleka said, pointing to a woman in a crowd of people, "I know her. She came to the Talawakelle temple with me." On crosschecking with the woman, the teacher found that Tillekeratne had indeed developed friendly relationships with that woman while worshiping at the local temple. On another occasion, Gnanatilleka pointed to a woman in a group and said, "She is angry with my Talawakelle mother." Again, on crosschecking with the woman, the teacher found that she was a neighbour of Tillekeratne's family. Although she had had some disagreements

with Tillekeratne's mother in the past, they had since patched up.

4. About a year after the controlled recognition tests, Stevenson crosschecked the full case, re-interviewing all the key people involved. His subsequent investigation uncovered that Tillekeratne had no sister named Lora or Dora but had had a girl-classmate named Lora. In 1970, Stevenson took her along with another woman to Gnanatilleka's house, unannounced. When he asked the now nearly fifteen-year-old Gnanatilleka if she could recognise the two women, she said that she did not know the second woman and identified Lora as "Dora," thus repeating her childhood confusion about the two names. She further added that she had known her in Talawakelle. This recognition was remarkable because Lora, who had been a teenager during Tillekeratne's life, was now an approximately thirty-year-old woman.

Overall, Gnanatilleka's recognitions are difficult to explain away as resulting from exaggerations because:

i. Her recognitions of several people were complemented by her exhibition of the appropriate emotions towards them.

ii. Statements of facts that she could not have known by appearance alone supplemented her recognitions of those people.

iii. Her correct recognitions were not only affirmative but also negative. She accurately stated that she did not know those individuals whom Tillekeratne had not known.

iv. Most importantly, her recognitions happened in carefully monitored conditions in the presence of several neutral observers.

All these factors combined make the explanation of exaggeration untenable for this case.

In many cases, the exaggeration explanation is further problematised if not plainly refuted by the phenomenon of birthmarks and birth defects.

BIRTHMARKS AND BIRTH DEFECTS

When Stevenson was approximately halfway through his over four decades of reincarnation research, he noticed that 35 percent of the children who recollected memories of a past-life also had birthmarks or birth defects whose location corresponded with wounds on the body of the previous personality.

Pursuing this research angle, Stevenson compiled a massive document, *Reincarnation and Biology*, which extended over two volumes, each more than one thousand pages. For several cases, he even presented eye-popping photographic evidence of the remarkable correlation between the birthmarks or birth defects and the fatal wounds.

This research angle pioneered by Stevenson has led to the discovery of many more cases with birthmarks or birth defects in various parts of the world.

Case with Double Birthmarks:
Titu Singh

Let's consider the case of Titu Singh that appeared in the London-based magazine, *Reincarnation International, Vol 1, No. 2,* and was broadcast in 1990 on the BBC TV news program *"Forty Minutes."*

Titu Singh was born in Lucknow. When he was two and a half years old, he began to talk of his other life in Agra, giving many specific details. He said that he had been the owner of a radio, TV, and video shop; his name had been Suresh Verma; he had a wife named Uma and two children. He also said that he had been shot and then cremated, and his ashes had been thrown in the river. Initially his parents ignored what he was saying. But when Titu repeatedly requested to be taken to Agra and even threatened to leave home alone to go there, his older brother decided to travel to Agra to check out his younger brother's claims.

To his amazement, Titu's statements turned out to be true. He found a video shop called Suresh Radio, which was run by a widow named Uma, whose husband Suresh had been shot dead. When Titu's brother approached Uma and explained the situation to her, she was initially taken aback but then decided to investigate by visiting the Singh family the next day.

When the Verma family arrived unannounced, Titu, who was outside washing at the tap spotted them and shouted to his parents that his "other family" had come. When his parents invited the visitors to sit in the veranda, Titu insisted that Uma sit next to him—an odd way for a five-year-old in India to relate to an unknown grown-up woman. Titu then astounded Uma by describing in detail a family outing to a fair in a neighbouring village where Suresh had bought her sweets, information that was known only to Uma and her deceased husband.

When Titu was taken to Agra, he correctly recognised Suresh's two children from among the many neighbourhood children playing together. In fact, the Verma family had arranged for his two children to play with other children as a ploy to test Titu, and he passed with flying colours. When Titu entered the video shop, he immediately and correctly identified the changes made to the shop after Suresh's death.

Most importantly, Titu accurately described how Suresh had been shot in the head at night while sitting in his car after arriving home from work. This was confirmed both by Uma and by Suresh Verma's autopsy report. The report stated that he had died from a bullet wound in the right temple. It also gave the exact size and location of the entry and exit wounds.

When they shaved Titu's hair, they saw one birthmark on each side of his head. These birthmarks were round, indented shapes whose location coincided exactly with the locations of the entry and exit wounds of the bullet that killed Suresh Verma.

The exaggeration explanation can't explain such birthmark cases because exaggerations can never produce a mark or a defect on the body, leave alone a congenital mark or defect, leave far alone marks whose locations coincide with fatal wounds on some deceased person's body.

Could these marks have originated in natural causes that had nothing to do with the past-life? Possibly.

Stevenson analyses this explanation in his book *Reincarnation and Biology*. He explains that the known natural causes for birthmarks and birth defects are genetic factors, viral infections during pregnancy, and chemical teratogens (substances like alcohol or thalidomide that interfere with normal embryonic development).

Yet medical researchers have found that these known causes account for only 50% of all birthmark and birth defect cases. Moreover, none of these known causes was found in a majority of the birthmark-reincarnation cases. Additionally, in some cases, it was definitively ascertained that no natural causes led to the birthmarks.

Let's look at one such case from Stevenson's book *Reincarnation and Biology* that involved a rare birthmark: a nasal polyp a small vascular growth on the surface of the mucous membrane of the nose.

Case with Rare Birthmark: Indika Ishwara

Indika and Kakshappa Ishwara were identical twins; that is, twins developed from the same fertilised ovum and so, having the same genetic material. Indika was born five minutes before Kakshappa on 24 October 1972 in Sri Lanka in a village about seven kilometres from the town of Weligama.

From the age of three, Indika started talking about a previous life in a town named Balapitiya that was nearly thirty miles from his hometown. He said that he had attended a large school in Ambalangoda, a bigger town near Balapitiya, adding that he would commute by train. He referred to his previous parents as his Ambalangoda mother and Ambalangoda father. He said he had been called "Baby Mahattaya," which meant "Little Master." He stated that he had an older sister named Malkanthie, with whom he had bicycled. He further mentioned an uncle named

Premasiri and a person he addressed as "Aunt Chilies." He said that his previous father wore trousers whereas his own father wore a sarong. He added that his previous home had electricity, whereas his present home didn't. He described his previous mother as darker, taller, and fatter than his present one.

Indika's family did not know anyone in Ambalangoda, but one of his father's friends worked there. Giving him the details provided by Indika, his father asked him to make enquiries. Those enquiries revealed a family that matched Indika's statements. Their oldest son Dharashana Samarasekera had succumbed to viral encephalitis when he was just ten, about four years before Indika's birth.

When Dharashana's father came to know about Indika, he became curious and paid an unannounced trip to Indika's hometown. He found his way to Indika's father's shop. While he waited there to be taken to the family's home, an employee asked him whether he had a son named Mahattaya and a daughter named Malkanthie, adding that Indika had been mentioning these names. On hearing this, Dharashana's father was amazed as this was true: his son Dharashana had been nicknamed "Baby Mahattaya" and his daughter was called Malkanthie. When he was brought to the house, Indika, on seeing him announced to his mother, "Father has come."

Subsequently, Indika, who was just four, was taken to Dharashana's house and Dharashana's family also came to meet him again. During these meetings between the two families it was discovered that as many as thirty-one of Indika's statements were true when applied to Dharashana.

One of Dharashana's uncles was named Premasiri; his full name was Sangama Premasiri de Silva. He had an aunt who had cooked chillies for him. Dharashana's father wore trousers and the family's home had electricity. Dharashana's mother's appearance matched Indika's description.

During Indika's second visit to Dharashana's house, he started searching for something outside a house in the family's compound. When he found it, he pointed it out. On the wall of a concrete drain was scratched the name *Dharashana* along with the date 1965. This had presumably been done by Dharashana at a time when the concrete was still wet. No one in Dharashana's family had noticed or known about the markings on the wall until Indika pointed it out.

Germane to our discussion is Indika's rare birthmark: a nasal polyp that his parents noticed when he was a year old. Nasal polyps are not unusual in later ages but they are quite rare in infancy. Moreover, Indika's identical twin did not have one. So his polyp can't be attributed to genetic causes. Then what caused it?

Significantly, during his illness, Dharashana had received both nasal oxygen and a nasal feeding tube. Could the irritation from one of those have produced the subsequent polyp in Indika? The nasal polyp may not be as dramatic as some of the unusual deformities arising from fatal wounds in the previous personality. But its significance is in its rarity and in its having absolutely no known natural cause—especially because an identical twin didn't have it.

The significance of the birthmarks is not just in the elusiveness of their natural cause but also in the precise correlation of their location with the previous personality's wounds.

Is the correlation all that precise? Could this seeming precision be a result of mere coincidence?

To find answers to these questions Stevenson divided the average-sized adult body into a grid of 160 boxes, each measuring ten centimetre square. By plotting the skin marks on this grid, he showed that the chance of the correspondence between the position of a birthmark and the position of a wound is just 1/160.

Moreover, many cases like those involving death due to fatal bullet wounds feature two birthmarks on the child's body corresponding with the two wounds—the entry wound and the exit wound—on the body of the previous personality. In these cases, the probability decreases to 1/160 x 1/160, or 1/25,600.

Let's consider a case that involved six correlating birthmarks from Ian Stevenson's book *Where Reincarnation and Biology Intersect*.

Case with Multiple Correlating Birthmarks: Necip Unlutaskiran

Necip Unlutaskiran was born in Adana, Turkey in 1951. On his birth, his mother noticed that he had seven birthmarks. When he was six, he started speaking about a previous life in Mersin, a city that was about 80 kilometres from Adana. He said his name in that life had been the same as in this life: Necip. He also stated that he had children whom he wanted to see. He further said that he had been stabbed and while describing the stabbing, he pointed to the parts of his body where he had birthmarks to indicate the places where he had been stabbed.

His parents ignored his statements for six years. But when his requests became insistent, his mother finally took him to a village near Mersin where her father lived with his second wife. Though Necip had never met his grandfather's second wife until then, on seeing her he suddenly said that he recognised her from his previous life in Mersin. There, she had known a man named Necip Budak and she confirmed the accuracy of Necip's statements about him.

When Necip expressed his now-intensified desire to go to Mersin, his grandfather took him there. He recognised several members of the family of Necip Budak, and those members confirmed the accuracy of Necip's statements about Necip Budak's life.

Necip Budak had been a quarrelsome person especially when drunk. Once, in a drunken state, he had begun teasing and then taunting an acquaintance, who, possibly drunk himself, had stabbed Necip Budak repeatedly with a knife. Necip Budak had collapsed on the street and rushed to a hospital where he had died the next day.

Among Necip's various statements, the most significant was his claim that he had once stabbed "his" (Necip Budak's) wife in the leg resulting in a lifelong scar. Necip Budak's widow did indeed have a scar on her thigh at the place where Necip had claimed to have stabbed her in his previous life.

Additionally, the twelve-year-old Necip also expressed emotions as if he were Necip Budak. He showed great affection toward Necip Budak's children and showed such attachment to Necip Budak's wife that, out of intense jealousy, he wanted to tear up her second husband's photo.

Most importantly, the locations of Necip's six birthmarks correlated with the locations of the knife wounds that had led to Necip Budak's death. The probability of six correlations is extremely low at $1/160^6$, making chance an unrealistic explanation.

For our analysis, these multiple birthmarks cases with their precise correlations are particularly difficult, if not entirely impossible, to be explained away as products of exaggeration.

To summarise, in this chapter we discussed two possible explanations for the cases of past-life memories: guesswork and exaggeration. The guesswork explanation is problematised by cases with memories that are specific, detailed, and accurate. The exaggeration explanation falls short in cases in which the:

1. Children's statements are documented in writing and crosschecked by the investigator before the meeting with the family of the previous personality.
2. Meeting with the previous personality is carefully supervised and objectively documented by the investigators.
3. Children have birthmarks and birth defects which have no known natural cause and whose locations correlate precisely with the locations of wounds on the previous personality's body.

If exaggeration also can't account for past-life memories, what other explanation remains? Might these accounts be massive frauds? We will analyse this in our next chapter.

CHAPTER THREE

PAST-LIFE MEMORIES—FRAUD BY PARENTS OR INVESTIGATORS?

"There are two ways to be fooled. One is to believe what isn't true; the other is to refuse to believe what is true."
—*Danish Philosopher Soren Kierkegaard (1813 – 1855)*

"It's one thing not to see the forest for the trees, but then to go on to deny the reality of the forest is a more serious matter.
—*Biologist Paul Weiss*

So far, we have seen how past-life cases cannot be adequately explained based on knowledge from normal sources, guesswork, or exaggeration. What other explanations remain? Could the cases be just elaborate frauds—orchestrated either by the parents or by the investigators? This was one of the foremost questions in the mind of Tom Shroder, an editor at the Washington Post, when he decided to investigate, journalistically, the past-life memories cases uncovered by Ian Stevenson.

Shroder travelled extensively with Stevenson in Lebanon and India to observe keenly and analyse critically these cases on the field of investigation: in the homes of the children and their relatives—both related to the present life and the previous life. Shroder went on to compile his first-hand reports about the case investigations into a fascinating book entitled *Old Souls: The Scientific Evidence for Past Lives.*

Among the many positive reviews that this book received, the review by the *Publishers Weekly* is typical: "The journalistic objectivity Shroder brings to his material makes this an exceptionally valuable treatment of an often disparaged subject." We will quote from Shroder's book as we analyse the possibilities of fraud. Let's look first at parental fraud and then at investigator fraud.

FRAUD BY PARENTS

The parental fraud explanation holds that the parents spin the entire story of a past-life memory and drill the child to perfection to play the critical part in the fraud. Stevenson, Tucker, and other past-life researchers have carefully analysed this possibility, and we present here a systematised summary of their analysis.

The fraud explanation begs the question: what would the parents gain by committing a fraud? The possible gains can fall in three broad categories: validation of personal beliefs, monetary benefits, or fame and prestige. In many cases, none of these gains is relevant. Let's see how:

1. **No Validation of Personal Beliefs**
   Might the parents be driven by the agenda to prove their personal belief in reincarnation to others? Perhaps, in some cases. But this agenda is entirely inapplicable to

the many cases found in America and Europe in which the parents didn't believe in reincarnation.

In fact, in many of these cases, the parents had been predisposed by their religious teaching and cultural upbringing to explicitly disbelieve in reincarnation, and so, would have had reason to expose a fraud if it occurred and not set one up themselves. And Tucker, who has focused on investigating cases primarily in America, has found a significant number of strong cases among such disbelieving parents.

Even in the cases in Asia and other places where the parents believe in reincarnation, validating their beliefs is not particularly important for the parents for they, as well as most of the people in their social circle, believe in reincarnation implicitly. Because the parents rarely find their belief in reincarnation challenged, which is the norm in more westernised societies, they don't feel any need to prove their belief, leave alone orchestrate a fraud to prove it.

During his investigations, Shroder confirmed this pattern of parental behaviour reported by Stevenson and other researchers. He wrote in *Old Souls*, "Family members admittedly interested in and open to the possibility of reincarnation had nonetheless refused to leap to any conclusions or embellish the child's statements. If anything, they had played them down."

Moreover, a widespread belief among Indians, especially rural Indians, is that those children who talk about their past-life will die young. Stevenson stresses that he has found no statistical basis for this belief—

the mortality rate of children who remember past lives is no higher than that of those who don't. Still, most rural parents continue to believe this and so, they often discourage their children from speaking about the earlier life even when the children want to. Therefore, it seems extremely unlikely that they would initiate a fraud that would require the child to speak about past-life memories repeatedly.

2. **No Monetary Benefits**

Stevenson and all subsequent past-life researchers follow a standard policy of not paying anything to the parents for conducting their interviews as they want to ensure that the case doesn't get corrupted; that is, the parents and other interviewees don't exaggerate or invent points in the hope of getting money. So there is no monetary gain for the parents in the investigation itself. In fact, the investigation that extends for hours and hours often constitutes a financial strain for some of the parents—especially those from financially challenged backgrounds who need to work throughout the day to make ends meet. Consequently, they sometimes even resent the precious long hours spent in giving exacting interviews to the researchers.

In some of the cases, a child born in a poor family believes himself or herself to be the reincarnation of a deceased member of a wealthy family. Might the parents be conniving such a relationship so that they can get some money from the wealthy family? Possibly. But general patterns in the detailed case histories show that even when the poor parents develop a relationship with the wealthy family during the course of the investigation, very rarely do these parents ask for gifts from the wealthy family— and even rarer are the occasions when they actually do get gifts.

So overall there's no monetary benefit for the parents in contriving these cases.

3. **No Fame or Prestige**

Might the parents be setting up the fraud to gain fame and prestige? Possibly. But again, detailed analysis of case patterns shows that in most cases the parents don't appear eager to publicise their child's past-life memories. Even when the children speak about a past-life, the parents, being believers in reincarnation, accept that their child must have been somebody in a previous life and don't bother about who he or she was. So they don't pay much attention to the details spoken by the child. In a few cases, the child requests repeatedly, and insistently to be taken to the arena of the previous lives and even threatens to go off alone if the parents do not take him or her there. Only in such cases do most parents start broadcasting the details to locate the previous personality.

Prestige as a driving motive of the parents is plausible in those few cases in which the child claims to be the reincarnation of a celebrity. Consequently, researchers always treat such celebrity reincarnation claims, whenever they occur, with extra scepticism. (Abiding by their spirit of reasonable scepticism, we have avoided discussing any celebrity cases in this book.) But most of the children with spontaneous past-life memories recall fairly normal lives as ordinary, little-known people. Such claims, even when proven to be true, don't bring any prestige at all.

Thus, in a majority of the cases, no tenable reason seems to exist for parents to commit a fraud. Additionally, there are two strong arguments that go against the fraud explanation.

4. **The Practical Difficulty in Executing a Fraud**
To pull off a fraud would involve:

i **Onerous drilling of the child**: The parents would have to drill the child, repeatedly and thoroughly, to make him or her repeat the same false story accurately, over and over again, and spontaneously feign the apt emotions that go along with the story. Such meticulous drilling would be extremely difficult and troublesome; but it might still be possible when the child is old enough to be drilled.

However, in many cases the children start speaking about past-life memories as soon as they learn to speak. This early age seriously problematises the fraud hypothesis, as Shroder points out in his book *Old Souls*: "That extraordinarily young age made the idea of some form of fraud almost unthinkable . . .. Believing that a child could learn and repeat complex, accurate biographies at an age when his peers are struggling to learn the names of colours is almost an absurdity."

ii. **Ensuring the collusion of multiple witnesses:** In many of the past-life-memories cases, more than a dozen witnesses report having heard the child's statements or seen the child's recognitions and emotions or both. Making all these people give a consistent, deceptive account would require not just fraud but a systematic and intricate conspiracy. As the parents don't gain anything tangible by proving that the cases are true, it seems extremely unlikely that they would go through the massive effort necessary to organise a conspiracy.

5. **The Displeasing and Embarrassing Behaviours of the Children**

Most importantly, in several cases the parents find the child's past-life memories displeasing and even embarrassing; they explicitly wish and try to make their child "normal." In such cases, the fraud explanation fails completely. Why would the parents set up a fraud by which they would lose face?

Let's look at two such cases.

Case with Embarrassing Behaviours: Ma Tin Aung Myo

(Stevenson, I. 1983. Cases of the reincarnation type, Vol. IV)

Ma Tin Aung Myo was born in Burma in 1953. When she was about four, walking with her father, an airplane flew overhead and she became mortally scared. Thereafter, every time a plane flew overhead she cried saying that she was frightened that the plane would shoot her. This behaviour continued for several years.

At about the same age, one day she suddenly started weeping. When asked the reason she replied that she was pining to return to Japan. Since then, she would frequently lie on her stomach and cry disconsolately, saying she felt homesick for Japan. She claimed to have been a Japanese soldier stationed in her family's village in Burma during World War II and had been killed by machine-gun fire from a low-flying Allied plane when the Japanese were retreating from Burma. Also, whenever Americans and Britishers were mentioned in her presence she would become angry.

Along with her phobia of planes and philia for Japan, Ma Tin Aung Myo also complained that the Burmese climate was too hot, a common complaint by Japanese soldiers stationed in Burma. She also disliked spicy Burmese food and preferred sweet foods. As a young child, she showed a marked liking for fish, particularly half-cooked fish. All these dietary inclinations were characteristic of the Japanese. Moreover, she also spoke words in a strange tongue that nobody around her could understand.

Additionally, she strongly identified herself as a male. When young, she habitually played with boys and loved to play the role of a soldier. She told her parents that she wanted to be a soldier and pressed them to buy toy guns for her to play with. She insisted on wearing boys' clothes so fervently that when her school authorities demanded she come to school in a dress, she refused to do so and dropped out of school at the age of eleven.

Her self-identification as a male continued into her adulthood, and she would ask others to address her as a male. Her father had died when she was young and her mother had looked after her thereafter. Her mother had strongly opposed her masculine dress and behaviour, yet she had persisted. Her mother had been worried about her bleak prospects of marrying a good man if she herself dressed like a man but Ma Tin Aung Myo had been unfazed. She had no intention of marrying a man, for she considered herself to be a man and wanted to marry a woman.

When she was twenty-seven years old, around the time when Stevenson last saw her family, he was told that she still aspired to become a soldier and continued to dress as a male. At that time she was living in another town with her steady girlfriend.

For our analysis, this case offers two significant pointers:

Her pining for Japan: When the Japanese had occupied Burma they had committed many atrocities there. So they were hated and feared by the Burmese. Since the Burmese had such an overwhelmingly negative attitude towards the Japanese, it is extremely unlikely that anyone in her Burmese surroundings would have induced Ma Tin Aung Myo's pining for Japan and her self-identification as a Japanese.

Her self-identification as a male: Ma Tin Aung Myo lived in a conservative third world country, Burma, at a time when its traditional culture was still socially influential. Such cultures strongly emphasise the importance of its members adhering to their conventional gender roles. Society strongly frowns upon any deviation from these gender roles. Those who deviate thus become a source of great embarrassment for their relatives. So it's unreasonable to posit that those very relatives—in this case Ma Tin Aung Myo's parents—would court such embarrassment by perpetrating a fraud.

Let's look at another case in which the child's memories were displeasing to the parents because they crossed religious boundaries and thereby threatened to trigger religious tensions.

Case with Displeasing Behaviour: A Muslim-to-Hindu Reincarnation

In an article in the *Journal of Scientific Exploration*, Vol 4, No 2, 1990, University of Virginia researcher Antonia Mills provides an overview of various cross-religious Indian cases, that is, Hindu-to-Muslim or Muslim-to-Hindu cases, and then provides a detailed analysis of one Muslim-to-Hindu case.

Mushir Ali Shah, the eldest son of the *Fakir* Haider Ali Shah through his second wife Najima, had lived with his parents in the town of Kakori, Lucknow, in Uttar Pradesh, India. He worked as a horse-cart driver carrying fruits or vegetables from Kakori to the market in Lucknow. On 30 June 1980, when he was approximately twenty-five years old, a tractor struck him and his mango-filled cart, killing him on the spot. The fatal accident occurred on the road from Kakori to Lucknow at a half-kilometre distance from the village of Baj Nagar.

In Baj Nagar, which is about five kilometers from Kakori, in April 1981 was born Naresh Kumar Raydas as the third of four children of Guru Prasad Raydas.

1. When Naresh started speaking at the age of two, he would often repeat, to his parents' puzzlement, the words *"Kakori, Kakori"* and also *"karka, karka,"* which means "horse-cart" in the local dialect.

2. Around the same age, he would kneel down at home as if to perform *namaz,* the Muslim form of ritual

prayer and would stop if he noticed that he was being observed.

3. The *Fakir* from Kakori, who maintained his family by begging alms and offering blessings, would come to Baj Nagar and to Naresh's house every Thursday. When Naresh learnt to walk, he would follow the *Fakir* to the next two or three houses and then return to his own home. Although his parents told him to address the *Fakir* by the Hindu term for a mendicant, *Baba*, he would address him as *Abba*, the Urdu word for father used by Muslims and some Hindus in that area of Uttar Pradesh.

4. By August 1987, when Naresh was about six, he would repeatedly say that he was a Muslim from Kakori. One day when he saw the *Fakir*, he again called him *Abba* and asked him, "Don't you recognise me? In my house there are five neem trees. I was hit by a tractor." He asked the Fakir to take him home, a request that the befuddled *Fakir* refused.

5. The next morning, Naresh compelled his mother to take him to the *Fakir's* house in Kakori. Once there, he led her unguided through a part of Kakori that neither he nor his mother had seen before, until they reached the *Fakir's* house.

There Naresh again called the *Fakir* "my *Abba*," and his wife Najima as *Ammi* (Mother). He also recognised Mushir's brothers and a sister who was present along with her husband, whom he called by his name—Mohammed Islam.

He asked Najima, "Where is my younger brother

Nasim?" When she told him that he was sleeping, Naresh went to him and woke him up. As Nasim was trying to gather his wits, Naresh hugged him and started kissing him.

When asked how many brothers and sisters he had, Naresh answered, "Five brothers, six sisters. One of the sisters is a stepsister." This was correct in relation to the time when Mushir was alive. When Najima pointed to her six-year-old daughter Sabiah who had been born three months after Mushir's death and asked who she was, Naresh replied, "She was in your stomach at that time."

6. Naresh also correctly identified Mushir's suitcase among the five metal suitcases inside the house and accurately described its contents before it was opened.

7. The *Fakir* and his wife also noted that Naresh had a slight depression near the middle of his chest at the same place as Mushir's chest wound from his fatal accident.

8. Naresh recognised many of the people from Kakori who had gathered at the *Fakir*'s house. He even asked the wife of a man named Zaheed whether she had returned to the *Fakir* the 300 Rupees that he had deposited with her husband. Mushir had indeed deposited that amount with Zaheed who had returned it three days after Mushir's death.

9. When the *Fakir's* family prepared to send Naresh back with five Rupees, he demanded, "What do you mean? That you will send me off without giving me tea and eggs?" Mushir had been very fond of tea and eggs, and

used to have them every day. Naresh's demand for eggs was significant because his family, being vegetarian Hindus, did not eat eggs.

For our analysis, the critical point of this case is that the two families belonged to two different religions that have had a long history of mutual tensions in India. So, neither of the families was interested in establishing any reincarnational connection with each other.

Mills explains in her article that in many of these cross-religious cases, both the Hindu and the Muslim families tried to suppress the child's speech and behaviour: "Hindu parents of a child who claimed to be a Moslem generally tried to take measures which they hoped would erase the child's previous-life memories. The techniques used included simply ignoring the child's claims, teasing, piercing the child's ear, turning the child on a potter's wheel, and taking the child to an exorcist out of fear that the child would go mad. One Moslem family tried a combination of rotating the child counter clockwise on a millstone (to "undo" his past-life memories), tapping him on the head, and beating him."

Naresh's case echoed this general pattern. Both the families desired to deny or at least downplay the case even if it existed— certainly not to invent one when it didn't exist. So they were unlikely to have given Naresh even any minor cues, leave alone have consciously orchestrated a major fraud.

Might Naresh's family have been interested in proving their belief in reincarnation? Possibly, but what interest would Mushir's family have had in joining the fraud? Their religion opposed belief in reincarnation. So if religious bias had played any role here, it would have made them deny or even disprove reincarnation.

Consequently, they would have exposed the fraud, not colluded on it. Mushir's parents accepted Naresh to be their son reincarnated *not because of their religious beliefs, but in spite of their beliefs*. They had been taught to disbelieve in reincarnation but the experience and the evidence made them give up their disbelief.

When the *Fakir* was asked about his response as the case had unfolded, he said that he had not believed in reincarnation before this case. During his weekly visit to Baj Nagar, when Naresh had identified himself as his son, he had felt deeply troubled. Unable to sleep that night he had prayed at midnight, "Allah, what is this mystery?"

The next day when Naresh came to his house and recognised several people and things correctly, he felt that Allah had solved the mystery for him: Naresh was indeed his son Mushir, reborn. Najima, though initially shocked that an unknown Hindu boy was claiming to be her son, soon became convinced by his many correct recognitions.

When they recounted these events, both of them were moved to tears and his voice trembled with emotion. Thus, the sheer force of the recognitions transformed their attitude towards reincarnation from disbelief to belief.

The reactions of Mushir's other family members were revealing and reflective of the general Muslim attitude towards reincarnation. Typical of their reaction was the response of Mushir's sister Waheeda. She described how Naresh had correctly identified her by stating, "You are my sister." But when asked about her conclusion from the recognitions, she replied bluntly, "We don't believe in reincarnation."

In general, what was typical among Muslims was not just denial of reincarnation but denial even of the permission to investigate the possibility of reincarnation. Researchers sometimes faced covert or overt opposition from the Muslim community when they attempted to investigate past-life-memories cases involving Muslim children.

Mills explains the exceptional feature of Mushir's case that enabled the investigation: "Perhaps it is because the *Fakir* was, and is respected as a Moslem holy man, that I found no opposition to the study of the case on the part of any of the numerous Moslems whom I interviewed regarding the case. This lack of opposition was not typical of the other Moslem and half-Moslem cases."

Thus, fraud seems to be entirely unlikely as a possible explanation in cross-religious cases like Mushir's. There are many other cases in which the parents found the behaviour of their children displeasing. For example, Stevenson, in his book *20 Cases Suggestive of Reincarnation*, describes the case of Jasbir Singh.

This boy, who was born in a lower-caste Hindu family, said that he was from a higher Brahmin caste and so, refused to eat the food cooked in his own house. In conventional Hindu practice, the Brahmins, in order to maintain their ritual purity, avoid eating food cooked by people of the lower castes. Jasbir was so convinced about his Brahmin identity and so adamant about not eating food cooked by anyone other than a Brahmin that his father had to get special food for him, cooked in a nearby Brahmin's house.

This spectacle went on for not one or two days but for a whole year and a half. Why would a father orchestrate a fraud that would embarrass him by forcing him to tell others that his own son refused to eat the food cooked in his own house—and by forcing him to request others to cook food for his son?

Even if we grant that the father might have had some unknown motive, how could he have willed his three-year old son into refusing to touch the food in his own home? How could he have prepared a child of that age to starve until he was provided food from another house?

At an age when most children wouldn't even have understood caste distinctions or the concept of impure and pure food, how could he have made a child ask insistently for pure food cooked by a high-caste family?

In another case investigated by Stevenson, a Muslim boy started walking toward a nearby village as soon as he learnt to walk. His parents had to repeatedly intercept him and bring him back. It was only later when he began to speak that he said that he was a Hindu boy in an adjacent village. Again, due to the cross-religious feature of this case, fraud is untenable as an explanation. But even if fraud had been theoretically tenable, it would have been practically impossible: how could the parents have made their son run towards an unknown village at an age when he couldn't even speak?

To conclude, the parental fraud hypothesis is rendered inadequate by the absence of any substantial incentives for the parents and the presence of many significant disincentives for them.

If the parents hadn't committed a fraud, might the investigators themselves have committed it?

FRAUD BY INVESTIGATORS

Ian Stevenson was the pioneer and foremost researcher in the field of past-life memories. Let's look at his motives and methods to analyse whether he might have perpetrated a fraud.

Stevenson had secured his MD in 1943 from McGill University in Montreal, graduating at the top of his class. By 1957, his expertise in his field led to his being appointed head of the department of psychiatry at the University of Virginia, School of Medicine at the relatively young age of thirty-nine. During his extensive reading done out of professional and intellectual interest, he came across forty-four cases of past-life memories, an overview of which he published in 1960.

Soon, he started getting invitations from various parts of the world to investigate similar cases. Sensing that pursuing this line of investigation might lead to significant scientific breakthroughs, he embarked on what was to become a lifetime of meticulous research into past-life memories. Fuelled by his tireless spirit of scientific enquiry, he risked his secure career, even giving up his position as the head of his department, to focus on past-life research.

Critical and Cautious Research Standards

Despite his passion for this unconventional field of research, Stevenson never sought publicity and focused more on compiling and evaluating evidence than on making sensationalist claims meant to grab headlines. He pioneered the introduction of methodological rigour in the empirical study of past-life memories.

One of his most important methodological decisions, one that has now become a standard for most serious researchers, was to focus on memories of children instead of older people. Stevenson reasoned that it is much easier to know the possible sources of knowledge of small children than of adults, so inferring whether a particular piece of information could have come from normal sources or not is much safer in children's cases than in adults' cases.

Due to his critical and cautious research standards, his findings were published several times in many reputed scientific periodicals including the *American Journal of Psychiatry* and the *International Journal of Comparative Sociology*. Moreover, the care and precision of his research won accolades from the most conservative sections of the academic world. Even the *Journal of the American Medical Association*, which is the pre-eminent medical journal in terms of size, influence, and tradition, stated that he had "painstakingly and unemotionally collected a detailed series of cases, in which the evidence for reincarnation is difficult to understand on any other grounds. He has placed on record a large amount of data that cannot be ignored." (1 December 1975 issue).

Noteworthy is the explicit acknowledgement of the absence of any research bias or any methodological laxity, leave alone any intentional fraud. The *Journal of Nervous and Mental Disease* devoted one issue (September 1977) almost entirely to Stevenson's work. Therein, psychiatrist Harold Lief lauded Stevenson as a methodical investigator and commented, "Either he is making a colossal mistake, or he will be known (I have said as much to him) as 'the Galileo of the 20th century'."

Vindication of Research Standards by a Neutral Third Party

As mentioned earlier, Shroder started his investigation of Stevenson's work as a sceptic. But he explains in his book *Old Souls* that after seeing first-hand the thorough empiricism of Stevenson's research methods and the undeniable authenticity of the memories, he found his scepticism impossible to sustain. When Stevenson passed away in 2007, the *Journal of Scientific Exploration* dedicated a full issue to his memory. Therein, Shroder wrote: "Neither self-delusion, intentional fraud, peer pressure, nor coincidence could explain how the children Ian investigated could have known all that they knew about strangers who'd died before they were born."

Consistently Similar Findings of Multiple Researchers All Over the World

Further discounting the fraud explanation is the fact that Stevenson is far from being the only researcher in the field. Scores of researchers with respectable academic credentials from various parts of the world have been investigating past-life memories for several decades. Some eminent researchers are Jim Tucker, Carol Bowman, Jürgen Kiel, Emily Williams Cook, Godwin Samararatne, Satwant Pasricha, Sybo Schouten, U Win Maung, Antonia Mills, and Erlendur Haraldsson, to name just a few.

Additionally, the cases of past-life memories number not just in dozens or hundreds but thousands. Explaining away all these cases as frauds seems grossly unreasonable. Certainly, some of the cases may be fraudulent but dismissing all of them thus violates the spirit of science to follow open-mindedly the evidence, wherever it takes one.

If investigator fraud is also not an adequate explanation for past-life memories, then what other explanation remains? We have already seen the inadequacy of explanations based on information by normal means, guesswork, exaggeration and parental fraud. The most plausible explanation left is the one offered by the children themselves: they had acquired those memories during their previous lives as the previous personalities—that is, they have reincarnated.

Of course, accepting the reincarnation explanation may require so major a conceptual overhaul as to make us sceptical. And no doubt a healthy dose of scepticism can protect us from uncritical acceptance. But an overdose of scepticism can trap us in uncritical rejection. We need to be sceptical not just about the evidence but also about scepticism. Scepticism can only tell us what is wrong, never what is right.

Conjuring a tenuous chain of coincidence, complicity, and conspiracy for one case is reason enough for pause. But cooking up the same flimsy chain for hundreds of cases points compellingly to intelligence held hostage by close-mindedness. German Philosopher Arthur Schopenhauer cautions, "The discovery of truth is prevented more effectively, not by the false appearance of things present and which mislead into error, not directly by weakness of the reasoning powers, but by preconceived opinion, by prejudice."

Francis Bacon, the seventeenth-century pioneer of the empirical approach that laid the foundations of subsequent scientific advancement outlines in his book *The New Organon and Related Writings,* the open-mindedness that is foundational for progress in knowledge: "The world is not to be narrowed till it will go into the understanding . . . but the understanding is to be expanded and opened till it can take in the image of the world as it is in fact."

Being open enough and bold enough to expand our understanding is indispensable to the ongoing progress of human knowledge. When we become ready to expand our understanding while examining past-life memories, we may well discover that we don't have to search in our imagination for a monumental tale because reality has a far more monumental insight in store for us.

Might we have under-estimated ourselves? Might there be more to us than our material bodies that are doomed to mortality? Might there be a hitherto-unknown energy-field associated with our personality that survives bodily death, and moves on to a new body? Might that unknown energy-field be what the great wisdom-traditions call the soul? Might that soul be the essence of who we are? This indeed is the best inference from the cases of children's spontaneous past-life memories.

With this chapter, we complete the analysis of spontaneous past-life memories started two chapters earlier.

Over the last three chapters we have reviewed nearly a dozen documented cases of past-life memories, discussed their four principal features—recollections, recognitions, birthmarks and birth defects, and behaviours—and analysed the inadequacy of four normal explanations: information by normal means, guesswork, exaggeration, and fraud.

Thus, these cases provide credible, if not compelling empirical pointers to the existence of a soul that reincarnates from one body to another.

In the next chapter, we will examine another area of research that points to the soul's capacity to exist separately from the body during this very life. That area is near-death experiences.

CHAPTERS 1-3 SUMMARISED AT A GLANCE:

Possible explanations for past-life memories	Why not possible?
Information from normal means	1. Knowledge of languages extinct for over a millennia e.g. the case of Harold Jaworski 2. Information too obscure to be known e.g. the case of James Leininger 3. Information too intimate to be known e.g. the case of Shanti Devi
Guesswork	Information too specific to be known e.g. the case of Nazih Al-Danaf
Exaggeration	1. Written record of memories e.g. the case of Ajendra Singh Chauhan 2. Precise recognitions under multiple supervision e.g. the case of Gnantilleka Baddewithana 3. Presence of birthmarks and birth defects e.g. cases of Titu Singh with his double birthmarks; Indika Ishwara with his genetically inexplicable nasal polyp; and Necip Unlutaskiran with his six correlating birthmarks

Fraud by parents	1. Most reincarnation-believing parents don't care for the validation of their beliefs—and many sceptical parents accept their children's accounts despite their disbelief, not because of their belief.
	2. Parents get no monetary benefits. On the contrary, many poor parents often have to lose their daily wages to go through rigorous, repeated interviews by researchers.
	3. Most parents don't get or seek fame or prestige.
	4. For the parents, orchestrating a fraud by drilling a small child to act deceptively and getting multiple witnesses to collude is often impossibly difficult.
	5. Why would parents make their children behave in ways that bring distress and embarrassment? e.g. the case of Ma Tin Aung Myo with her cross-dressing and trans-gender self-identification e.g. the communally volatile case of Naresh Kumar Raydas identifying himself as Mushir Ali Shah e.g. the case of Jasbir Singh with his refusal to eat the food cooked by his "lower caste" parents

Fraud by investigators	1. Stevenson's research standards acknowledged in top mainstream scientific journals such as the *Journal of the American Medical Association, American Journal of Psychiatry, the Journal of Nervous and Mental Disease* and *the International Journal of Comparative Sociology.* 2. Stevenson's research rigour appreciated by sceptical investigative journalism e.g. Tom Shroder's book *Old Souls* 3. Multiple researchers all over the world have uncovered consistently similar findings

CHAPTER FOUR

NEAR-DEATH EXPERIENCES

*"Science may keep saying: 'Such things are simply impossible';
yet so long as the stories multiply in different lands,
and so few are positively explained away, it is
bad method to ignore them."*
—William James, *Essays in Psychical Research*

Whereas past-life memories point to the existence of something—a soul?—that can move from one body to another over multiple lifetimes, near-death experiences (NDEs) point to the existence of something that can, within the same lifetime, move out of the body and return to it.

NDEs are the extraordinary perceptions of physically unconscious people who were close to death, often due to cardiac arrest or other life-threatening conditions. These people returned from the brink of death to give us their amazing testimonies.

In typical NDEs, subjects after falling unconscious,

- See themselves leaving their body
- Observe their body and its vicinity from an out-of-body perspective generally from above an operating table
- Feel themselves floating away from the vicinity, sometimes through a dark tunnel to some other-worldly realm

In that realm, they

- See or interact with some persons such as their religion's sacred icons or deceased relatives
- Feel a profound sense of peace
- See flashing in front of their eyes, a review of their life wherein they see the good and bad they have done
- Are told to or decide to return to their bodies
- Find themselves returning back to consciousness, sometimes mysteriously healed

Much of the depiction of NDEs in the popular media focuses on the subjects' journey to otherworldly realms and the visions therein. Fascinating as these features may be, they are not empirically provable or disprovable.

The most scientifically interesting aspects of NDEs are those features in which the patients report having seen their body from a point outside themselves and also give objective descriptions of, say, the surgical procedures adopted by the medical staff. Such objective perceptions can easily be checked against what really happened, which makes them very useful in evaluating the authenticity of the NDEs.

The claim of the near-death experiencers (NDErs) that

they saw themselves from outside their bodies raises the question: How could unconscious people observe themselves from outside of their bodies?

FIRST POSSIBLE EXPLANATION: HALLUCINATIONS?

Could NDEs be nothing more than hallucinations? The wishful thinking of people who want to ignore their fear of death? It's possible, in some cases.

NDEs are markedly different from hallucinations in their contents and effects, as explained in the table below:

Hallucinations	NDEs
Hallucinations generally comprise of disorderly events with hazy visions	NDEs generally comprise of orderly events with clear perceptions
Hallucinations usually leave their subjects feeling disturbed and agitated	NDEs usually leave their subjects feeling peaceful and serene
Hallucinations have little noteworthy long-term effect on the subjects	NDEs are often profoundly life-transforming, inspiring the subjects toward a more purposeful and spiritual reorientation of beliefs and lifestyle.
Hallucinations are often caused by anorexia or lack of oxygen, which leads to confusion	NDEs occur in situations where there is no lack of oxygen and are frequently characterised by great mental clarity, often clarity greater than that during normal consciousness.

Some hallucinations are caused by hypercarbia or excess carbon dioxide.	Most documented NDEs have occurred in hospitals and even in the hospitals' operation theatres and intensive care units – all places where excess carbon dioxide is extremely unlikely.
Some hallucinations originate from the hallucinogenic drugs that the subjects had taken.	Many NDEs have happened to people when their medical condition was carefully monitored and they had no intake of hallucination-inducing drugs.

Indeed, NDEs do not appear to be attributable to any specific physiological cause as most hallucinations can be.

In an article in the medical magazine *The Lancet*, Pim van Lommel and his Dutch co-researchers highlight the fatal flaw in any physiological explanation of NDEs: "With a purely physiological explanation [for NDE] such as cerebral anoxia [absence of oxygen], for the experience, most patients who have been clinically dead should report one." In simpler words, if physiological conditions cause NDEs, then all people under those conditions should have NDEs. Yet only some do. This selectiveness of NDEs suggests that they are not caused by physiological conditions alone.

SECOND POSSIBLE EXPLANATION: GUESSES BASED ON PRIOR GENERAL KNOWLEDGE?

Yet another fact about NDEs counters their equalisation with hallucinations even more convincingly: that fact is the factuality of their perceptions. Many people who have had NDEs are able to provide information—factually accurate information—about things that happened while they were unconscious. Their accounts are so detailed and so true to life that there is no way they could have been merely hallucinating.

Let's consider one case reported by pioneering NDE researcher Michael Sabom in his book *Recollections of Death: A Medical Investigation.*

A retired Air Force pilot who had suffered a massive heart attack later recounted his resuscitation in great detail. He even described the two needles of the defibrillator, an electronic device used to administer electric shock to restore the normal functioning of the heart: "It [the defibrillator meter] was square and had two needles on there, one fixed and one which moved . . . The first needle moved each time they punched the thing and somebody was messing with it. And I think they moved the fixed needle and it stayed still. It [the moving needle] seemed to come up rather slowly, really. It didn't just pop up like an ammeter or a voltmeter or something registering. The first time it went between one-third and one-half scale. And then they did it again, and this time it went up over one-half-scale, and the third time it was about three-quarters."

Sabom explains the significance of this specific observation: "I was particularly fascinated by his description of a 'fixed' needle and a 'moving' needle on the face of the defibrillator as it was being charged with electricity. The movement of these two needles is not something he could have observed unless he had actually seen this instrument in use. These two needles are individually used,

(1) to preselect the amount of electricity to be delivered to

the patient [patient's description: "they moved the fixed needle and it stayed still"] and

(2) to indicate that the defibrillator is being charged to the preselected amount [patient's description: "the moving needle seemed to come up rather slowly, really. It didn't just pop up like an ammeter or a voltmeter or something registering"].

This charging procedure is only performed immediately prior to defibrillation since once charged, this machine poses a serious electrical hazard unless it is correctly discharged in a very specific manner. Moreover, the meters of the type described by this man are not found on more recent defibrillator models but were in common use in 1973 at the time of his cardiac arrest."

How could a person who was (1) in the middle of a cardiac arrest (2) about to be jolted by an electric shock (3) while being almost certainly unconscious (4) not in a physical position to observe the defibrillator meter (5) methodically observe the motion of the needles on its dial?

Could these be the products of educated guesses?

That was indeed the opinion of Sabom, an American cardiologist who, as a sceptic started researching NDEs in the late 1970s. In *Recollections of Death*, he outlines his initial plan to discredit what patients who had had out-of-body experiences claimed to have seen.

"I would pit my experience as a trained cardiologist against the professed visual recollections of lay individuals. In so doing, I was convinced that obvious inconsistencies would appear, which would reduce these purported visual observations to no more than an 'educated guess' on the part of the patient."

But Sabom's initial scepticism soon faded away as evidence piled up over three decades of NDE research. Going back to the

Air Force pilot case mentioned earlier, could the information about the medical procedure have come from his prior general knowledge? It's unlikely that such precise details could have been a part of the general knowledge of patients not directly connected with the medical profession.

Sabom decided to evaluate this possibility, anyway. He questioned a control group of twenty-five cardiac patients whose backgrounds were similar to the backgrounds of those patients who had reported NDEs. The control subjects were asked to imagine what they would see in an operating room where doctors were trying to resuscitate someone in cardiac arrest. Two of the subjects could not give any description at all. Twenty of the remaining twenty-three made major errors.

In stark contrast, of the 32 subjects who reported having NDEs, 26 gave general descriptions that did not include major errors. Six gave detailed reports that matched their medical records exactly—medical records they had not seen. Based on this study, Sabom concluded, "These NDE accounts, most likely, are not subtle fabrications based on prior general knowledge."

The idea that the NDErs' accounts might be derived from prior general knowledge is further challenged by another fact: many of them described not just standard surgical procedures but also distinct events that happened specifically during their own cases.

In another one of Sabom's cases, the subject provided a detailed and medically accurate description of her lower back surgery. And she reported that her surgery had been performed to her surprise, not by her surgeon but by the chief resident in neurosurgery. That detail was correct but no one had told her about it.

Sabom is not the only researcher to have come across NDEs involving factual perceptions. An article published in *The Journal of Scientific Exploration* by E.W. Cook and his colleagues describes the case of Al Sullivan.

Al Sullivan had an out of body experience on 18 January 1988 during emergency coronary quadruple bypass surgery at Hartford Hospital, in Hartford, Connecticut. Sullivan reported that during the surgery, while his chest was held open by metal clamps, he had seen one of the surgeons, Dr. Hiroyoshi Takata, do something peculiar—he flapped his elbows as if trying to fly.

When asked about this, Takata admitted that during surgeries he would often hold his palms together over his chest, and use his elbows to point at things around the room. After scrubbing in, Takata did not want to touch anything until he was actually ready for the surgery, so he would give instructions to the nurses by pointing with his elbows. From a distance, those movements could certainly seem like flapping. Another surgeon who had been present that day, Dr. LaSala, confirmed that during this particular surgery Takata had actually flapped his elbows just as Sullivan had described.

As many as 107 such cases with correct perceptions excerpted from 39 publications by 37 different authors or author teams have been summarised by Janice Miner Holden in the article "Veridical Perceptions in Near-death Experiences" in the compilation *The Handbook of Near-death Experiences*. These cases provide even more evidence that NDE subjects do indeed provide factually accurate information from their experiences. How do these patients see what they say they've seen?

Might they have been partially conscious?

THIRD POSSIBLE EXPLANATION:
PARTIAL CONSCIOUSNESS?

Why Only Sights?

Normally, when a person gradually loses consciousness, the visual sense shuts down before the auditory sense. So, if the NDErs' perceptions occurred when they were partially conscious, they should have reported what they had heard, not what they had seen. But most NDE perceptions consist primarily of sights, while some consist of sights only, no sounds at all.

Sights Imagined Through Sounds?

Maybe the visual images they describe are fabricated. Maybe what they think they saw was only imagined after having heard the sounds in the operating room. Maybe they are just repeating what they've overheard the doctors and nurses say. Is that possible? Let's consider by examining specific cases.

One of Sabom's subjects reported seeing himself getting a shot in his right groin. Actually, the doctors were drawing blood for a test. Then why did he mistake it to be a shot?

If he had manufactured the image based on something he'd overheard, he probably would not have made that mistake. But such a mistake, Sabom analysed, would be natural for someone who had simply seen what happened. Visually, drawing blood and giving an injection look quite similar: both involve inserting a needle.

Sights Imagined Through Touch?

Could this particular image have been reconstructed not from what the patient heard but from what he felt? The medical reports said that blood had been drawn from his left groin, but the subject reported that he had been "given a shot" in the right groin. If his description had been manufactured based on what he had felt, he should have felt the prick of the needle in his left groin and he would have said so. But if the subject had been looking down at his body from above as he described, he would have seen, from his perspective, the needle going into the right side of his body.

Paranormal Perceptions?

The idea that subjects concoct visual impressions from what they've heard or felt is further refuted by NDE cases in which subjects describe accurate paranormal perceptions, perceptions that could not have come from any of their senses. In some cases, subjects provide accurate information about things, events, or persons outside their immediate vicinity, information that they could not have obtained even if they had been conscious.

Sabom records a case in which a patient recovering from illness suffered an unexpected cardiac arrest. After he was revived he reported an out-of-body experience in which he had travelled down the hall and seen his wife, eldest son, and daughter arriving at the hospital. They had indeed arrived at the precise time he had gone into cardiac arrest.

At the time of the incident, the patient was due to be discharged soon. He was not expecting his family members to visit, but even if he had known they would be visiting him, he couldn't have known exactly who would be there because he had six grown children who took turns accompanying their mother when she came to see him. His family members were standing in the hall, ten doors away from the room where doctors were trying to resuscitate him. Moreover, his face was pointed away from his relatives. Given all these conditions, it seems unlikely that he could have seen their arrival by any normal means.

A similar case was documented by Dr. Kimberley Clark, a professor of medicine at the University of Washington in the book *The Near Death Experience*. She reported the case of a migrant worker named Maria who had undergone treatment for cardiac arrest.

After Maria had been resuscitated, she told Clark about her NDE in which she had found herself floating above her body, looking down at the doctors and nurses. She even described an object she had seen outside the hospital at a location to which she had no access. She told Clark that while she was outside her body, she had "thought herself" out of the hospital and up the outer wall to another floor. There she had come "face-to-face" with a tennis shoe sitting on a window ledge. Maria had been admitted at night and had been completely incapacitated ever since.

Naturally intrigued by her claim of having seen a shoe, Clark went outside the hospital and looked up at the window ledges but could not clearly see anything from so far down. Next, Clark went back inside the building and up to the third floor. She investigated room after room, having to press her nose against the narrow windows to see outside. Finally, she found the shoe and retrieved it. She was shocked to note that the minute details Maria had given about the shoe were both completely correct and impossible to see from inside the hospital. Only someone somehow suspended by the ledge could have noted those details. How could Maria have come to know about them especially in her condition, completely immobile and near death?

How can what such subjects saw be explained by the idea of partial consciousness? Even if they had been fully conscious, they would not have been able to see what they've described. Perhaps the most logical explanation is the one offered by the subjects themselves: They left their bodies and observed what was going on from that perspective.

In 1954, Hornell Hart published a study of those out-of-body experiences during which the subject reported having perceived something that required some kind of paranormal knowledge. Hart collected 288 cases from various publications and determined that in 99 of these cases, the information given by the subject was later confirmed. These kinds of NDEs involving verified paranormal perceptions have been reported for over half a century. They are being reported with even greater frequency today.

How Can the Blind See?

In their book *NDEs of the Blind: Mindsight*, Kenneth Ring and Sharon Cooper describe several blind subjects who were able to see only during their NDEs and never again. One of these subjects, forty-five-year-old Vicki Umipeg, was born blind, her optic nerve completely destroyed at birth due to being given too much oxygen in the incubator. Yet, during two NDEs, she was able to see quite clearly. These two experiences were the only two times in her life she was able to see.

How can the partial consciousness hypothesis explain such cases? Even if the subjects had been partially conscious during their NDEs, this can't in any way explain their visions because they had no vision whatsoever even when they were fully conscious.

Perceptions During Documented Unconsciousness?

In the *Lancet* article mentioned earlier, Pim van Lommel and his colleagues described a remarkably accurate perception experienced by a person who had been in a coma when brought to the hospital.

A nurse removed his dentures as a part of the resuscitation procedure and kept them nearby. For ninety minutes, the staff vigorously tried to revive him, after which he developed sufficient heart rhythm and blood pressure but remained comatose. He spent more than a week in the ICU before he came out of his coma.

When the nurse who had removed his dentures came to give him his medication, he immediately told her to bring his dentures, which had somehow gotten lost while he was being resuscitated. In spite of the fact that he had been unconscious at the time, he correctly described the cart on which she had placed the dentures, even mentioning the many bottles on it and the sliding drawer underneath. He also gave accurate descriptions of the small room where he had been resuscitated, and of the attire and looks of those present at the time. Finally, he told her that while watching his lifeless body from above, he had been terrified that the medical staff seemed inclined to stop resuscitating him. The nurse confirmed the man's perception, stating that they had been pessimistic about his prognosis because his condition had been so poor when he was admitted.

How could a person who was already deep in a coma when brought to the hospital and who remained unconscious for more than a week after resuscitation, have accurately described what happened at a time when the medical staff were desperately trying to bring him back to life?

More research, conducted in 2001 by Sam Parnia and his team, at the University of Southampton offers a formidable challenge to any physiological or pharmacological explanations of NDEs. For a full year, the team meticulously monitored every patient admitted to the city's General Hospital and resuscitated after suffering a heart attack.

They focused on patients who were clinically dead with no pulse, no respiration, and dilated pupils for varying amounts of time before they were brought back to life. Through independent EEG studies, it is known that for patients in this condition, the brain's electrical activity and therefore all brain function shuts down. And yet, 11 percent of the patients who survived their cardiac arrest recalled having emotions and perceptions while unconscious.

After decades of cautious research, Parnia, who, like Sabom had started researching NDEs as a sceptic declared: "What is clear is that something profound is happening. The mind—the thing that is 'you' - your 'soul' if you will—carries on after conventional science says it should have drifted into nothingness."

One of the most amazing cases of a NDE during documented unconsciousness is that of Pam Reynolds, reported by Sabom in his book *Light and Death*. While suffering clinical brain death, Pam was still able to perceive accurately the things happening around her.

Pam Reynolds was diagnosed with a giant basilar artery aneurysm: a weakness in the wall of the large artery at the base of her brain had caused that artery to balloon. A fatal rupture could have come at any moment. Initially, her doctors offered her no hope of survival. But eventually she came in touch with neurosurgeon Dr. Robert Spetzler at the Barrow Neurological Institute in Phoenix, Arizona. Spetzler was a specialist who was at that time pioneering a rare, dangerous but sometimes necessary technique called hypothermic cardiac arrest, or "Operation Standstill." This daring operation required that the patient's body temperature be lowered to 60 degrees Fahrenheit, her heartbeat and breathing stopped, her brain waves flattened, and the blood drained from her head.

Spetzler explains, "If you would examine that patient from a clinical perspective during that hour, that patient by all definitions would be dead. At this point there is no brain activity, no blood going through the brain. Nothing, nothing, nothing."

During this period of clinical brain death, Pam had a vivid NDE in which she saw—with clarity and detail—her head, the cranial saw, the operating room, and the doctors and nurses there. She was surprised to see the peculiar way in which her hair had been shaved and was alarmed to see someone cutting her groin area during what was supposed to be brain surgery. From the area where her legs were, she also heard a female voice saying that the blood vessels were too small on the right side and a male voice suggesting that they try the other side.

It's incredible that during this period of brain death, she had any perception at all. But it's even more incredible that she could have heard the two voices. During the entire time, not only was she under general anaesthesia but also had special earpieces moulded into her ears. Those tiny speakers were emitting 90 to 100 decibel clicks at a rate of 11 to 13 clicks per second. Sound at that volume is easily louder than a whistling teakettle and nearly as loud as a lawn mower or even a passing subway train. This sound was meant to monitor her most basic level of brain function and ensure that she was deeply and consistently anaesthetised.

Just imagine tiny speakers specially moulded to completely fill the ear canal and emitting clicks that loud and rapid. Then imagine the likelihood of accurately hearing a brief conversation that was taking place at the volume of a normal conversation—about 60 decibel, substantially below the 90 to 100 decibel clicks. Even though the conversation was happening a few feet away, there's little possibility it could have been overheard. Regardless, even if Reynolds had somehow been partially conscious and hearing things as she normally would, it's strange that she never mentioned hearing clicks, much less feeling distracted by them or struggling to hear through them.

Spetzler summarises the profound questions raised by Reynolds' NDE: "At that stage in the operation, nobody can observe, hear, in that state, and I find it inconceivable that your normal senses, such as hearing, let alone the fact that she had clicking modules in each ear, that there was any way to hear [what she heard] through normal auditory pathways. I don't have an explanation for it. I don't know how it's possible for it to happen, considering the physiological state she was in. At the same time, I have seen so many things that I can't explain, that I don't want to be so arrogant as to be able to say that there's no way it can happen."

When Reynolds was asked how she was able to hear, she replied that it was through nonphysical processes.

All of these cases—involving accurate perceptions beyond one's vicinity, among the blind, and among those with no brain activity—show that partial consciousness fails to explain NDEs.

And if partial consciousness is not an explanation, what other explanation remains? Perhaps all these reports are merely the products of fraud.

FOURTH POSSIBLE EXPLANATION: FRAUD?

Could these cases be misreported or completely made up by the subjects or the researchers?

While fraud could possibly account for a few cases, how could it explain the sheer frequency and consistency of NDEs? Thousands of subjects and hundreds of researchers from all parts of the world have reported remarkably similar NDEs.

Could the subjects be lying about what they perceived? Maybe, but what would they gain? Most people who have NDEs gain nothing by describing what they've seen or heard. In fact, in most cases, they are met with the scepticism of the doctors and nurses and even their own families.

Might they be seeking attention and fame? Possibly, in a few cases. But many NDErs, fearing a sceptical response, don't speak out about their NDEs unless encouraged by others. This reluctance to speak up makes it unlikely that all of them are lying to seek attention or fame.

Some NDErs do see their religious beliefs validated by their experiences, and they seek to publicise their NDEs to attract the faithful. Still, even their speaking about their NDEs in itself doesn't explain the experiences themselves, especially if they had reported accurate perceptions at times when they were known to be medically unconscious. And seeking fame doesn't apply to the many NDErs who have reported accurate perceptions while unconscious and haven't publicised their experiences, only reported them to researchers who enquired.

Moreover, NDErs across the world report experiences that share many similar patterns such as movement out of the body, perception from an out-of-body perspective, and journey to some otherworldly realm. To claim that NDErs who haven't known each other have somehow colluded to report similar experiences seems to stretch scepticism.

And even if somehow such global collusion had occurred, how could it have co-opted into its cause children who are not even in their teens? Several children have reported factually accurate perceptions that have withstood scrutiny by researchers. To say these children too somehow colluded, is to stretch scepticism to extremism.

Then what about the researchers themselves? Could they be fabricating the evidence? Again, possible in a few cases. But NDE research is not the monopoly of a few renegade scientists; hundreds of scientists all over the world are involved. In fact, these scientists have formed several global forums such as *The International Association for Near-Death Studies* (IANDS) that examines the physical, psychological, social and spiritual nature, and ramifications of near-death experiences. The credibility of IANDS is evident from the calibre of its publications: its quarterly newsletter *Vital Signs* and its peer-reviewed *Journal of Near-Death Studies*. In such professional research scenarios, wherein errors and deceptions are weeded out through critical scrutiny by a community of researchers, the very fact that NDE research has not only survived as a field of serious scientific study but also flourished bears testimony to its credibility.

Writing in the classic, exhaustive anthology *Irreducible Mind: Towards a Psychology for the 21st Century*, Emily Williams Kelly, of the University of Virginia, points out, "That [Deception] is certainly always a possibility to be guarded against in individual cases; but when this suggestion is used repeatedly, and without supporting evidence as a blanket defense against the entire body of evidence, it should be recognized for what it is, which is simply an unwillingness to examine that evidence in a truly scientific spirit."

In this chapter, we discussed several cases of accurate perceptions of the near death experiencers that resist all normal explanations like hallucinations, prior general knowledge, partial consciousness, and fraud. Therefore, the most logical explanation for NDEs is the one offered by the subjects themselves: They were outside of their bodies when they made the observations that they later reported to others. Thus, these cases offer persuasive evidence for the idea that something non-physical—the soul, perhaps?—exists separate from the body.

After having examined over the last four chapters the empirical evidence for the existence of something non-physical, we will next examine whether the idea of a non-physical core has any theoretical basis.

CHAPTER SUMMARY AT A GLANCE:

Possible explanations for accurate perceptions in NDEs	Why the explanation doesn't work?
Hallucinations	NDEs are different from hallucinations in content, cause and effect How are near-death experiencers (NDErs) able to have accurate perceptions?
Prior General Knowledge	Why can't those who don't have near death experiences give as accurate descriptions as do NDErs? How can NDErs describe events specific to their treatments?
Partial Consciousness	Why do the perceptions primarily comprise sights? Are the perceptions imagined through sounds? No Are the perceptions imagined through touch? No How can NDErs perceive things beyond normal ranges of perception? How can the blind see during NDEs? How do NDErs perceive when their brain is absolutely inactive?

Fraud	How can NDErs, including even children, from various parts of the world report NDEs with similar core features?
	How can researchers from the world over, with respected credentials and working in a peer-reviewed environment, report for decades, cases that survive rigorous intellectual scrutiny?

CHAPTER FIVE

THE MYSTERIOUS PHENOMENON OF CONSCIOUSNESS

"Conscious experience is at once the most familiar thing in the world, and the most mysterious. There is nothing we know about more directly than consciousness, but it is extraordinarily hard to reconcile it with everything else we know."
–David J. Chalmers, The Puzzle of Conscious Experience, Scientific American, Dec 1995

What exactly is consciousness?

The phenomenon of consciousness eludes precise scientific definition. But before we get into technicalities, let's look at things intuitively. That intuition plays an important role in acquiring knowledge is recognised by Albert Einstein: "The intuitive mind is a sacred gift and the rational mind is a faithful servant."

INTUITIVE UNDERSTANDING

We can begin to understand consciousness as our sense of 'I'-ness—"I am," "I exist," "I am aware of my own existence," "I am aware of the world around me," and so on. But who exactly is the "I" that is aware?

Is it the body? Or is it something distinct from the body?

Let's consider five good reasons that intuitively suggest the "I" is distinct from the body.

1. Who Perceives?

When we see a flower or hear music, who is it that sees and hears? Is it the eye that sees? Is it the ear that hears? A dead body has eyes and ears. But it doesn't see or hear. Why?

Then, is it the brain or maybe the nervous system that sees and hears? Later we will analyse in detail at why brain functions alone don't explain consciousness. For now, suffice it to say that a dead body also has a brain and nervous system but it doesn't see or hear. Why?

Might the perceiving be done by something or someone distinct from the body?

2. Who is the Owner of the Body?

When we refer to the parts of our body, we say "My hand," "My legs," and so on, not "I hand," or "I legs." This suggests that "my hands" and "my legs" are different from "me."

The same is true of the body as a whole. We also say "my body" not "I body."

This difference between "me" on one hand, and "my body," "my hands," and "my legs" on the other, is not just a matter of semantics. We are not quibbling with words. It's also a matter of practical experience—

we *feel* ourselves to be the owner of our body, and its parts.

The question, then, still remains: who is the "I" that claims owners' rights over the body and its parts?

3. **Who's Gone?**

When someone dies, the way people speak about it can be quite telling. They say, "He has passed away" or "She's gone." But who passed away? What's gone? The body of the person they knew is still lying there; it has not gone anywhere. And yet they feel an acute sense of loss, as if their loved one has gone away. Their feeling of loss is not wrong: the person they cared for is certainly gone.

So the question remains: who's gone? When that person was there, the body was alive. But now that he or she is gone, the body is dead. Could that person somehow be independent of the body?

4. **When the Body Changes, Who is the I That Remains the Same?**

At every moment, from conception in the womb till death, our body is constantly changing. That's a scientific fact. In his book *The Science of Near-death Experience* Pim Van Lommel explains, "Our cells may be seen as our body's physical building blocks, yet every day some fifty billion cells in our body are broken down and regenerated. This is the equivalent of 500,000 cells per second. Every two weeks all of the molecules and atoms in our body's cells are replaced . . . And yet we experience our body as a continuity. How can we explain this experience of continuity of the ever-changing body?"

The question raised by Lommel is profound: How is it that despite such constant and total changes in our body, our sense of identity or "I"-ness remains unchanged? Your body changes, but you remain yourself. How?

5. **Am I Just a Bag of Chemicals?**

Your body is made up of various chemicals: carbon, nitrogen, calcium, phosphorous, potassium . . . Does that sound like you? Is that the stuff that makes up your identity, your personality?

Your body is made up mainly of water. When you think about who you are, do you think of yourself as a liquid? Or as watery? Between birth and death, thousands of gallons of water will go into and out of your body. The water comes and goes, but you are still here.

If we analyse the chemicals that make up the human body, measure the amount of each one, and then calculate how much they cost, the total doesn't add up to the average person's cost of living for even a day. Is that your net worth?

Just before and just after the moment of death, the chemical composition of the body remains the same. And yet something essential has changed.

What is that?

Could it be that something nonphysical is the source of life, and that something has left the body at death?

***

After these five intuitive reflections, let's now see what science has to say about consciousness.

PROBLEMS WITH MATERIALIST THEORIES ABOUT CONSCIOUSNESS

"Science's biggest mystery is the nature of consciousness. It is not that we possess bad or imperfect theories of human awareness; we simply have no such theories at all. About all we know about consciousness is that it has something to do with the head, rather than the foot."
—Physicist Nick Herbert, Quantum Reality: Beyond the new physics.

Today, many scientists approach the universe in strictly materialist terms; that is, they consider matter the only reality. These scientists generally see the universe, in all its variety and complexity, as merely the interplay of atomic particles functioning according to natural laws. Unsurprisingly therefore, many neuroscientists believe that consciousness emerges from the electrochemical activity of the nerve cells in the brain. But materialist explanations of consciousness have been challenged by several eminent neuroscientists. Nobel Laureate neuroscientists such as John Eccles, Wilder Penfield, and Charles Sherrington hold that a complete explanation of consciousness requires at least some consideration of non-material aspects.

This openness to exploring non-material explanations echoes the conclusion of another Nobel Laureate physiologist Albert Szent-Gyorgi, given in *Biology Today*: "In my search for life, I ended up with atoms and electrons, which have no life at all, and somewhere along the line, life has run out through my fingers. So, in my old age, I am now retracing my steps."

Why are so many eminent scientists considering a serious reassessment of the materialist approach to explaining consciousness? Well, when examining the idea that the brain is solely responsible for producing the phenomenon we call consciousness, at least three fundamental questions remain unanswered:

- How can brain cells, which are themselves unconscious dead matter, produce consciousness?
- How do our memories stay intact despite the constant regeneration of our brain cells?
- How can consciousness change the structure of the brain as observed in neuroplasticity?

1. How can Unconscious Brain Cells Produce Consciousness?

This problem has perplexed modern science right from the seventeenth century when the materialist approach first started gaining prominence.

In the nineteenth century, consciousness still remained a problem, as noted by English biologist T.H. Huxley in his book *The Elements of Physiology and Hygiene*: "How it is that anything so remarkable as a state of consciousness comes about as the result of irritating nervous tissue, is just as unaccountable as the appearance of the Djin when Aladdin rubbed his lamp."

And even now, in the twenty-first century nearly four hundred years since scientists started struggling with this problem no explanation has been found, as admitted in the special 125th anniversary issue of *Science* published in 2005. That issue of this reputed publication of the American Association for the Advancement of Science featured 125 questions that scientists were at that time unable to answer. The second most important unanswered question, after the question "What is the universe made of?", was, "What is the biological basis of consciousness?" In that special issue, science writer Greg Miller framed the problem in this way: "How [can] a particular pattern of photons hitting the retina produce the *EXPERIENCE* of seeing say, a rose."

Why is the simple act of seeing a rose such a difficult thing to explain? When we see a rose, light rays of various frequencies enter the retinas of our eyes. The eye cells react to the amount of light entering and then generate electrochemical impulses that pass through the optic nerve to the visual areas of the brain. This activates certain nerve cells and their connections with other cells.

What happens next? How does the image of a rose emerge in our consciousness? *Where* does the *experience* of seeing and feeling take place? *Who* is it that *sees* the rose? And who is it that *feels* the unique emotions associated with such an experience?

When confronted with such perplexing questions, some scientists claim that somehow or the other brain cell activity alone gives rise to the experience of seeing, the sense of "I-ness," and, in general, the whole phenomenon of consciousness.

But other scientific researchers have pointed out that the activities of brain cells and our conscious experience of emotions are two very distinct things. This is explained by astrophysicist Piet Hut and philosophy professor Bas van Fraassen, both from Princeton University, in the *Journal of Consciousness Studies:*

"If I've ever seen an incompatible pair of concepts, it's a configuration of molecules and a conscious experience! Life 'emerging' out of lots of molecules; consciousness 'emerging' out of lots of nerve cells. Well, why not consider time as 'emerging' out of clocks? Without clocks, no accurate time measurements. And a good clock provides excellent correlations with the flow of time. But time surely does not 'emerge' out of a clock."

Colin McGinn, a philosophy professor from the University of Miami, highlights the problem in reducing the ineffable complexity of conscious experience to simple brain activity: "The brain processes held to constitute conscious experience consist of physical events that can exist in the absence of consciousness. Electricity in the brain correlates with mental activity, but electricity in your TV presumably does not—so how can electrical processes be the essence of conscious experience?" (New Statesman magazine, 20 Feb 2012)

The fundamental feature of consciousness that differentiates it from brain cell activity and so stalls all materialist explanations is stated emphatically by neuroscientist Stevan Harnad in the *Journal of Consciousness Studies* (Volume 7, Number 4, 1 April 2000), "The problem is clear, hard, and staring us informally in the face: *I HAVE FEELINGS*." This is technically called as the hard problem of consciousness.

Thus a detailed study of the brain offers no adequate explanation on how it could possibly produce consciousness. Still, that's not the only problem with a purely materialist approach.

2. How Do Our Memories Stay Intact Despite the Constant Regeneration of Our Brain Cells?

It had long been believed that once we reach adulthood, we can never grow new brain cells. However, cutting-edge research has forced re-evaluation of this belief. A team of scientists from Harvard University, the Salk Institute, and the Sahlgrenska University Hospital in Sweden reported in the journal *Nature Medicine*, ". . . Cell genesis occurs in human brains, and . . . the human brain retains the potential for self-renewal throughout . . . life."

In a *New York Times* article neuroscientist Dr. Elizabeth Gould of Princeton University, who was one of the pioneers of this discovery, explained the serious questions it raised: "People believed that in order to store memories for a lifetime, you need a stable brain. If cells are constantly dying and new ones being produced, how would that be possible?"

Imagine that you wrote a message on a piece of paper and then you were able to one by one, gradually replace the molecules that make up that piece of paper. Suppose you completely replaced all the molecules and found that the new paper still had the same message written on it. Wouldn't that be incredible?

Of course, this is a simple example for illustrating the extremely complex and largely unknown mechanism that links memories and brain cells. But its simplicity notwithstanding, it highlights the problem that confronts any mechanism as consciousness researcher Dean Radin points out in his book *Conscious Universe*: "All of the material used to express that pattern [of information] has disappeared, and yet the pattern still exists. What holds the pattern, if not matter? This question is not easily answered by the assumptions of a mechanistic, purely materialistic science."

This question is actually so difficult to answer that it was also mentioned in *Science's* list of the key 125 unanswered questions. And the answer remains elusive despite enormous strides in brain research during recent years. Perhaps a more productive approach might be to re-consider the materialist assumptions that make the problem so difficult to solve.

Is it possible that our memories are stored not just in the brain but also somewhere else, possibly in a place somehow independent of the material body from where they are made available to the new brain cells? Might this imply that consciousness has its origin somewhere beyond the brain? Of course, it's true that damage to the brain usually impairs the functioning of the body. Damage to the speech centre of the brain, for example, often results in an inability to speak. But do such instances prove that the brain is the source of consciousness? Not necessarily. They demonstrate that the brain and consciousness are intimately connected but don't specify the nature of that connection.

Renowned psychologist William James postulated that the correspondence between brain damage and impaired bodily function could still be explained if we assume that the brain is merely transmitting, not producing consciousness. To illustrate this, he gave the example of the way a prism transmits light. When a prism is damaged, the light passing through it may be distorted.

Similarly, when the brain is damaged, consciousness passing through it may be impeded. A more contemporary example can be the relationship between a computer and its user. If the processor, the part of the computer responsible for running programs, somehow gets damaged, then the user won't be able to perform basic functions, and his or her ability to run programs, analyse data, and so on would be impeded. If the brain were akin to a processor for consciousness, then damage to a particular brain area would prevent the conscious self from performing the bodily functions associated with that area.

This idea of consciousness being in at least some ways independent of the brain finds support in one astonishing discovery: Some people are able to perform normal conscious activity despite having little or no brain.

"Is your brain really necessary?" That was the provocative title of an article published in the December 1980 issue of *Science*. The article reported the surprising findings of neurologist John Lorber of the University of Sheffield, a former member of the Nobel Prize Committee.

Lorber had earlier written in a scholarly journal *Developmental Medicine and Child Neurology* (December, 1970) about two children suffering from acute hydranencephaly, a congenital disorder in which cerebrospinal fluid is present not *around* the brain but *instead* of the brain. Normally, children with this disorder don't live for more than a year and even then, with brain functions severely impaired. But these two children, despite having no cerebral cortex whatsoever, were in all other respects normal.

In subsequent studies, Lorber found multiple cases in which people with less than 5% brain matter had IQs greater than 100, well within the average. The most dramatic case Lorber encountered involved a young student from the University of Sheffield itself: "There's a young student at this university who has an IQ of 126, has gained a first-class honors degree in mathematics, and is socially completely normal. And yet the boy has virtually no brain. When we did a brain scan, we saw that instead of the normal 4.5-centimeter thickness of brain tissue between the ventricles and the cortical surface, there was just a thin layer of mantle measuring a millimeter or so. His cranium is filled mainly with cerebrospinal fluid."

Lorber is not alone in reporting such findings. French physician Gustave Geley for example, reported similar cases in his book *From Unconscious to Conscious.* From the early part of the twentieth century, several anomalous cases have been documented of people who, despite having brains so severely damaged as to be practically inoperative, functioned quite normally.

And today, an extremely rare form of brain surgery seems to support Lorber's findings. Charles Choi reports in the *Scientific American* (24 May 2007), "The operation known as hemispherectomy—where half the brain is removed—sounds too radical to ever consider, much less perform. In the last century, however, surgeons have performed it hundreds of times for disorders uncontrollable in any other way. Unbelievably, the surgery has no apparent effect on personality or memory." If the brain is the source of consciousness, how could removing half the brain have no effect on things as fundamental as memory or personality?

For many years, surgeons have been removing small diseased parts of the brain without significantly affecting patients' memory. This is sometimes attributed to redundancy in the storage capacity of the brain; that is, the same memories may be stored in more than one place. So, the theory goes, even if part of the brain is lost, memories can be retrieved from elsewhere. Though this sounds plausible, the idea that as much as 50% of the brain is redundant—as hemispherectomy implies—is more difficult to believe. And some of Lorber's subjects had normal memories despite having less than 5% of the brain matter typical of an adult human brain. To account for this, neuroscientists would have to claim that 95% of the brain is redundant, a claim that is clearly unreasonable.

Cases like these support the possibility that consciousness may originate from beyond the brain.

Yet another finding challenges the claim that consciousness is a mere product of the brain: thoughts have been found capable of changing the structure of the brain itself.

3. How Does Consciousness Alter Brain Cells?

A number of scientific studies have demonstrated that normal mental processes can cause changes in the structure of the brain. This phenomenon is called neuroplasticity and its discovery stunned the mainstream scientific world. Why? Because, up to that point, most scientists had generally assumed that consciousness was a byproduct of the functioning of the brain. As a byproduct it should have had no capacity to affect the brain, its source. At that point in time, the power of thought to impact one's sense of well-being and one's general health had been well-known, but the power of thought to change the physical structure of the brain had hardly even been considered.

Psychiatrist Norman Doidge, in his *New York Times* bestseller *The Brain That Changes Itself* gives inspiring accounts of many patients who cured severe brain disorders by changing their thought habits, even though their disorders had been deemed incurable by conventional means. Changes in their thought patterns actually led to the formation of new connections in their brain cells, which in turn restored them to normal health.

Neuroplasticity is also documented in the book *The Spiritual Brain* by neuroscientist Mario Beauregard and science journalist Denys O' Leary. They report that many studies have shown how trust and positive expectations can bring about an actual biological change in the brain.

Norman Doidge explains that these findings are "the most important alteration in our view of the brain since we first sketched out its basic anatomy, and the workings of its basic component, the neuron. Like all revolutions, this one will have profound effects."

One profound effect, of course, is the re-evaluation of the claim that consciousness is a mere byproduct of brain function. As Pim Van Lommel observes, "It would be incorrect to claim that consciousness can only be a product of brain function. How can a product have the ability to change its own producer?"

If consciousness is not produced by the brain, then it stands to reason that it could have an existence independent of the brain. This idea is substantiated by the experiments of Nobel Laureate Dr. Wilder Penfield, documented in his book *The Mystery of the Mind.*

Penfield conducted several experiments designed to investigate the relationship between simple physical activities, such as raising or lowering one's arm, and the corresponding activities that happened in the brain.

At first Penfield observed that when a subject was told to raise his or her arm, a specific part of the cerebral cortex was activated. And when the subject was told to lower the arm, that part of the brain was deactivated.

Next, Penfield observed that when he used electrodes to artificially activate that specific part of the brain, the subjects' arm rose automatically. When Penfield asked the subjects, "Did you raise your arm?" the reply came, with conviction: "I didn't raise my arm; you raised it." When Penfield deactivated that part of the brain, the arm went down. Again, the subjects were sure that that this had happened without their personally doing anything about it.

Exactly what are the implications of this simple experiment? In both cases, activating and deactivating the brain led to the raising or lowering of the subjects' arm. But who or what was responsible for activating and deactivating the brain?

In the second part of the experiment, it was Penfield, an external agent, who physically stimulated the brain and caused the subjects' arm to react correspondingly. But in the first part, who was the agent responsible for stimulating the brain when the subject raised his arm voluntarily?

Penfield conducted several other experiments that demonstrated that no stimulation could ever make the subjects feel they were the ones responsible for raising their hands, regardless of which part of their brain was stimulated. To put it another way, wherever he looked in the brain, Penfield could not find the person, the individual conscious presence responsible for telling both the brain and the arm to act.

After more than four decades of research, Penfield concluded in *The Mystery of the Mind*, "The brain is a computer . . . But it is programmed by something that is outside itself."

Echoing this point, Pim Van Lommel in his book *Consciousness Beyond Life* quotes another Nobel Laureate, Sir John Eccles, "The brain is the messenger to consciousness."

To conclude, the claim that the brain alone produces consciousness is theoretically and empirically open to question because:

- Our memories are unaffected by the regeneration of the brain cells.
- Some people can function normally despite having a fraction of the total brain matter they are expected to possess.
- Thoughts have the power to change the structure of the brain.
- The individual conscious entity responsible for making the decisions that cause the body to move cannot be found anywhere in the brain.

All these points strongly suggest that consciousness has its own existence distinct from the brain, and that consciousness is not a product of the brain, but is its user. The brain is the tool for consciousness. If consciousness does indeed exist separately from the brain, then it could also exist separately from the body, as near-death experiences and past-life memories suggest.

In this book, chapters one to five have focused on establishing the theoretical and empirical tenability of the concept of reincarnation for our present scientific age. In the next chapter, we will explore the tenability that reincarnation has enjoyed throughout world history.

CHAPTER SIX

REINCARNATION IN WORLD HISTORY

"Transmigration, dating back to a remote antiquity, and being spread all over the world, seems to be anthropologically innate."
—M'Clintock and Strong's Cyclopaedia of Biblical, Theological and Ecclesiastical Literature

Reincarnation is sometimes thought of as a belief system peculiar to Eastern religious traditions like Hinduism and Buddhism. The fact however, is that the principle of reincarnation has enjoyed global intellectual appeal and widespread mass acceptance throughout most of known human history. Let's look at the prevalence of belief in reincarnation, first in the world's major civilizations and then in the world's major religions.

GREEK CIVILIZATION

The Greek civilization, which is the basis of most of modern Western civilization, had many prominent proponents of reincarnation. The best known among the early Greek advocates was the great mathematician and philosopher Pythagoras (circa 570 – 495 BC)

Pythagoras

Pythagoras stated, "Souls never die, but always on quitting one abode pass to another. All things change, nothing perishes. The soul passes hither and thither, occupying now this body, now that . . . As a wax is stamped with certain figures, then melted, then stamped anew with others, yet it is always the same wax. So, the Soul being always the same, yet wears at different times different forms."

Pythagoras didn't just propound reincarnation; he also described his past lives. Diogenes Laertius, whose writings were the key surviving sources for the history of Greek philosophy, stated, "He [Pythagoras] was accustomed to speak of himself in this manner: that he had formerly been Aethalides, and had been accounted the son of Mercury; and that Mercury had desired him to select any gift he pleased except immortality. Accordingly, he had requested that, whether living or dead, he might preserve the memory of what had happened to him. While, therefore, he was alive, he recollected everything; and when he was dead, he retained the same memory.

"At a subsequent period, he passed into Euphorbus, and was wounded by Menelaus. While he was Euphorbus, he used to say that he had formerly been Aethalides; and that he had received as a gift from Mercury the perpetual transmigration of his soul; so that it was constantly transmigrating and passing into whatever plants or animals as he pleased; and he had also received the gift of knowing and recollecting all that his soul had suffered in hell, and what sufferings too are endured by the rest of the souls.

"But after Euphorbus died, he said that his soul had passed into Hermotimus; and when he wished to convince people of this, he went into the territory of the Branchidae, and going into the temple of Apollo, he showed his shield which Menelaus had dedicated there as an offering.

"For he said that he, when he sailed from Troy, had offered up his shield which was already getting worn out, to Apollo, and that nothing remained but the ivory face which was on it. He said that when Hermotimus died he had become Pyrrhus, a fisherman of Delos; and that that he still recollected everything, how he had formerly been Aethalides, then Euphorbus, then Hermotimus, and then Pyrrhus. When Pyrrhus died, he became Pythagoras, and still recollected all the circumstances I have been mentioning."

Orpheus

Prior to Pythagoras, Orpheus, the legendary musician, poet, and prophet who founded the Orphic mystery religions taught that the body holds as a prisoner the immortal soul, which aspires for and achieves freedom after reincarnating over many lifetimes.

Socrates & Plato

After Pythagoras, Socrates (circa 470 – 399 BC) was the most prominent proponent of reincarnation, as can be inferred from the various writings of his foremost student, Plato. Reincarnation is a recurrent theme in many of Plato's works including the Republic, Phaedrus, Meno, Timaeus, Laws, and Phaedo.

"I am confident that there truly is such a thing as living again, that the living spring from the dead, and that the souls of the dead are in existence."

–Socrates, as quoted in Plato's *Phaedo*

"Every man's soul has, by the law of his birth, been a spectator of eternal truth, or it would never have passed into this our mortal frame, yet still it is no easy matter for all to be reminded of their past by their present existence."

–Socrates, as quoted in Plato's *Phaedrus*

ROMAN CIVILIZATION

After the Greeks came the Romans, who focused more on worldly advancement than metaphysical insight. Nonetheless, reincarnation continued to find advocates even among them.

Cicero

The reputed statesman and orator Cicero (106 – 43 BC) said in his book *Scipio's Dream*, "Know that it is not thou, but thy body alone, which is mortal. The individual in his entirety resides in the soul, and not in the outward form. Learn, then, that thou art a god; thou, the immortal intelligence which gives movements to a perishable body, just as the eternal God animates an incorruptible body."

Ovid

The poet Ovid (43 BC – 17 AD) said, "Nothing perishes, although everything changes here on earth; the souls come and go unendingly in visible forms; the animals which have acquired goodness will take upon them human form"

Plotinus

The Roman philosopher Plotinus, who was the leading representative of Neo-Platonism (205 – 270) wrote, "Such things . . . As happen to the good without justice, as punishments or poverty or disease, may be said to take place through offences committed in a former life."

Reincarnation continued to be taught in the Platonic Academy for over nine centuries till the time of Plato's last successor, Damascius, who taught it till 529 A. D. In that fateful year, the Christian Emperor Justinian persecuted Damascius and shut down the Academy. Thereafter, as Europe became increasingly Christianised, the teaching of reincarnation slowly went underground.

EUROPEAN CIVILIZATION—PRE-GREEK

The Druids

The Druids were members of the priestly class in North-Western Europe. They lived during the Iron Age and perhaps even earlier. Their fearlessness in the face of death was so extraordinary that Caesar investigated and noted its cause in his Gallic Wars (Book VI, 14; Translation William A. MacDevitt):

"They wish to inculcate this as one of their leading tenets, that souls do not become extinct, but pass after death from one body to another, and they think that men by this tenet are in a great degree excited to valor, the fear of death being disregarded."

Author Manly P. Hall, in his book *Reincarnation—The Cycle of Necessity* offers amazing information about the depth of the Druidic belief in reincarnation: "In the British Museum are receipts and other Druidic legal remains proving that it was not uncommon for these men to borrow money on their promise to repay in a future existence."

CHINESE CIVILIZATION

Reincarnation had eloquent proponents in China long before the spread of Buddhism there. Lao-Tze (600 BCE), the great Chinese writer of the classic *Tao Te Ching* and widely considered the founder of Taoism, taught reincarnation to his inner circle of students. He said, "To be ignorant that the true self is immortal, is to remain in a grievous state of error, and to experience many calamities by reason thereof." That Taoism accepts not just the eternality of the self but also its reincarnation is evident from Taoist records that depict Lao Tze appearing repeatedly on earth as different persons at different times.

Chuang Tzu, the influential Chinese intellectual who lived *circa* 4th century BCE, wrote, "Birth is not a beginning; death is not an end."

Similarly, Po Chu-I, the reputed eighth-century Chinese intellectual and poet of the Tang Dynasty, expresses his belief in reincarnation in an evocative verse:

> "After I depart, I cast no look behind
> Still wed to life, I still am free from care.
> Since life and death in cycles come and go,
> Of little moment are the days to spare.
> Thus strong in faith I wait, and long to be
> One with the pulsings of eternity."
>
> –Po Chu-I. 800 A. D.

AFRICAN CIVILIZATION

In his book, *Primitive Culture* (Chapter 12), English anthropologist Sir Edward Tylor describes the Yorubas, who are one of the largest ethnic groups in West Africa, ". . . Greeting a new-born infant with the salutation, 'Thou art come!', [they] look for signs to show what ancestral soul has returned among them."

Ghanaian researcher K K. Brakatu Ateko wrote in *The Canadian Theosophist, Jan – Feb 1962* about North African outlooks towards death: "Death was not looked upon as an enemy to be feared and propitiated. If one died, he was believed to have been born on the other side of the veil and vice versa in the case of birth in our world."

Similarly, researcher and author E. G. Parrinder wrote in the *Hibbert Journal (1 April 1957)* under the title *Varieties of Belief in Reincarnation*: "In tropical Africa, belief in rebirth is deeply enrooted."

AUSTRALIAN CIVILIZATION

Baldwin Spencer and F. J. Gillen state, in *Northern Tribes of Central Australia*: "In every tribe without exception, there exists a firm belief in the reincarnation of ancestors. Emphasis must be laid on the fact that this belief is not confined to tribes such as the Arunta, Warramunga, Binbinga, Anula, and others, amongst whom descent is counted on the male line, but is found just as strongly developed in the Urabunna tribe, in which descent, both of class and totem, is strictly maternal."

In the same vein, J G Frazer asserts in his book, *The Belief in Immortality and the Worship of the Dead*, "Belief in the rebirth or reincarnation of the dead was formerly universal among the Australian aborigines."

AMERICAN INDIAN CIVILIZATION

In his book, *The Soul of the Indian*, researcher Charles Eastman wrote: "Many of the Indians [of the United States] believed that one may be born more than once; and there were some who claimed to have full knowledge of a former incarnation."

Similarly, in *The Myths of the New World*, author Daniel G. Brinton, states that belief in reincarnation "was in fact one of their most deeply-rooted and widespread convictions, especially among the tribes of the eastern United States. It is indissolubly connected with their highest theories of a future life, their burial ceremonies, and their modes of expression . . ."

MODERN THINKERS

After this brief survey of the belief in reincarnation in the world's various ancient civilizations, let us now see what some eminent thinkers of the modern era have had to say about reincarnation.

"The soul comes from without into the human body, as into a temporary abode, and it goes out of it anew . . . it passes into other habitations, for the soul is immortal."
–Ralph Waldo Emerson, *Journals of Ralph Waldo Emerson*

"I did not begin when I was born, nor when I was conceived. I have been growing, developing, through incalculable myriads of millenniums . . . All my previous selves have their voices, echoes, promptings in me . . . Oh, incalculable times again shall I be born."
–Jack London, *The Star Rover*

"There is no death. How can there be death if
everything is part of the Godhead? The soul never
dies and the body is never really alive."
–Nobel Laureate Isaac Bashevis Singer,
Stories from Behind the Stove

"He saw all these forms and faces in a thousand
relationships . . . become newly born. Each one was mortal,
a passionate, painful example of all that is transitory. Yet
none of them died, they only changed, were always reborn,
continually had a new face: only time stood between
one face and another."
–Nobel Laureate Herman Hesse, *Siddhartha*

"Do you have any idea how many lives we must have gone
through before we even got the first idea that there is more
to life than eating, or fighting, or power in the Flock? A
thousand lives, Jon, ten thousand! . . . We choose our next
world through what we learn in this one . . . But you, Jon,
learned so much at one time that you didn't have to go
through a thousand lives to reach this one."
–Richard Bach, *Jonathan Livingston Seagull*

"As we live through thousands of dreams in our present life,
so is our present life only one of many thousands of such lives
which we enter from the other more real life . . . and then
return after death. Our life is but one of the dreams of
that more real life, and so it is endlessly, until the
very last one, the very real the life of God."
–Count Leo Tolstoy

After looking at the thoughts of eminent modern thinkers, let us turn to the world's major religious traditions, Western and Eastern, and see what they have to say about reincarnation. Let's begin by examining the position of reincarnation in the three Western or Abrahamic religions—Judaism, Christianity, and Islam.

JUDAISM

The Hebrew Bible, the main scripture of the Jews, is silent about reincarnation. This is in keeping with the overall tenor of Jewish tradition to focus on ethical behaviour in this world and view next-worldly subjects like reincarnation as a mystery unfathomable in this life. Nonetheless, a mystical side of the tradition known as Kabbalah helps seekers to cautiously and gradually fathom those mysteries.

For example, the *Zohar*, a foundational Kabbalah text, states, "The souls must re-enter the Absolute, from whence they have emerged. But to accomplish this end they must develop the perfections; the germ of which is planted in them. And if they have not developed these traits in this one life, then they must commence another, a third, and so forth. They must go on like this until they acquire the condition that allows them to associate again with God."

Many esteemed Kabbalists, who were also influential in mainstream Judaism, have fully endorsed reincarnation. Prominent among them are Abraham Abulafia (1240 – 1290); Joseph Karo (1488 – 1575); Moses Cordovero (1522 – 1570); Yitzhak Luria (1534 – 1572); Hayim Vital (1543 – 1620); Israel Baal-Shem Tov (1700 – 1760, the founder of the Hasidic movement); Moshe Hayim Luzzatto (1707 – 746); and Yahuda Ashlag (1886 – 1955).

Thanks partly to its advocacy by several such Kabbalists, belief in reincarnation did not stay restricted to esoteric mystics within Judaism but spread even to popular religious culture. Thus it is that in *The Dybbuk,* a much-loved play based on Jewish folklore, one character exclaims, "The souls of the wicked return in the form of beasts, or birds or fish—or plants even—and are powerless to purify themselves by their own efforts. They have to wait for the coming of some righteous sage to purge them of their sins and set them free."

Rabbi Menasah ben Israel, the somewhat eccentric yet esteemed theologian of the 15th century emphasises the centrality of reincarnationist belief to Judaism:

"The belief in the doctrine of transmigration of souls is a firm and infallible dogma accepted by the whole assemblage of our Church with one accord, so that there is none to be found who would dare deny it . . . Indeed, there are a great number of sages in Israel who hold firm to this doctrine so that they made it a dogma, a fundamental point of our religion. We are therefore dutybound to obey and accept this dogma with acclamation . . . as the truth of it has been incontestably demonstrated by the Zohar, and all books of the Kabbalists." (Quoted in *Reincarnation: The Phoenix Fire Mystery* by Joseph Head and S L Cranston).

The 16th-century Italian Kabbalist Hayim Vital, more formally known as Rabbi Hayim Vittal Calibrese, expounded on reincarnation in the Jewish mystical tradition over a full book: his philosophical masterpiece, *Sefer (or Sha' ar) HaGilgulim,* (The Gate of Reincarnation).

Thus, it can be concluded that reincarnation is certainly compatible with Judaism.

CHRISTIANITY

Anyone who reads the Bible will find that it neither explicitly advocates nor directly rejects reincarnation, a stand similar to its stand on the doctrine of the Trinity.

What is important is that some verses like Matthew (17:9-12) and John (9:1-2) do discuss reincarnation without rejecting it as heretical.

That reincarnation was a socially discussable notion during Jesus' time is evident from John (9:1-2): "And as Jesus passed by, he saw a man which was blind from his birth. And his disciples asked him, saying, Master, who did sin, this man or his parents, that he was born blind?"

The second alternative offered here by the disciples is easily intelligible: the parents sinned, so they had to suffer by having a blind son. But what are we to make of the first alternative: the man was born blind because of his own sins? When could he have committed those sins? In the womb? What possible sin could he have committed there? Crossed his legs wrong? Would his disciples, many of whom would be future apostles, be asking about such an absurd alternative? Surely they are asking whether the man had committed sins in some previous existence before his birth, an alternative derived from the doctrine of reincarnation, which was well-known during those times.

What was Jesus' response? If Jesus had wanted to teach that reincarnation was an error, a heresy, here was an ideal opportunity. How did he answer? In the next verse he says,

"Neither hath this man sinned, nor his parents: but that the works of God should be made manifest in him." Jesus avoids commenting on either of the alternatives but brings in a different angle: the man has been born blind so that Jesus may show a miracle, as he does after a few verses.

Can Jesus' answer be considered a universal philosophical explanation? Are all blind people freed from their blindness by miracles? Clearly not. So, through this incident, Jesus is not teaching an overarching philosophical truth but is demonstrating an exceptional divine grace.

Now let's consider this incident in the light of the universal biblical teaching: as ye sow, so shall you reap. If a person is born blind, his blindness is the way he is reaping what he has himself sown. When could he have sown that? The only sensible answer is: in an earlier life.

Overall, Jesus' response in this incident is typical of the entire biblical stand on reincarnation: neither deny it, nor emphasise it. If we couple this silence with the fact that Jesus and his followers lived in an Israel that largely accepted the doctrine of reincarnation, then it's reasonable to equate the silence with tacit acceptance.

Moreover, there are repeated references in the Bible to the return of prophets. For example, the Gospels refer to the prophecy about the return of the prophet Elijah no less than ten times.

And there are several references to reincarnation in the writings of many early Church Fathers who are recognised as authorities on the Bible: Clement of Alexandria (AD 150 – 220), Justin Martyr (AD 100 – 165), St. Gregory of Nyssa (AD 257 – 332), Arnobius (fl. 290), and St. Jerome (AD 340

– 420), to name a few. Even the famous St. Augustine (354 – 430), in his well-known book, *Confessions*, seriously considered reincarnation as a feature of the Christian worldview: "Did my infancy succeed another age of mine that dies before it? Was it that which I spent within my mother's womb? . . . And what before that life again, O God of my joy? Was I anywhere or in any body?"

Though reincarnation was widely accepted in the first two centuries of Christian history, over the next few centuries, it was banished from Christianity. The long and sad history that led to this is documented in many books such as the exhaustively researched *Reincarnation in Christianity* by Geddes MacGregor, a Christian theologian, and Emeritus Distinguished Professor of Philosophy at the University of Southern California. Let's briefly look over that history.

1. The famous Christian theologian Origen (AD 185 – 254) was one of the strongest proponents of reincarnation in Christian history. Origen was no fringe thinker in Christian theology; he has been acclaimed in the Encyclopaedia Britannica as "the most prominent and prolific of all the Church Fathers (with the possible exception of St. Augustine)" and glorified by Christians of great stature like St. Jerome, the translator of the Latin Vulgate, who proclaimed him "the greatest teacher of the Church after the Apostles" and St. Gregory, Bishop of Nyssa who honoured Origen as "the prince of Christian learning in the third century."

2. Three centuries after Origen, Emperor Justinian (483 – 565), his other accomplishments notwithstanding, used Christianity as a political tool to solidify his hold on his

subjects. He rationalised that if people were told that they had only one life to perfect their lives, then that would impel them to be "good Christians" and thus good citizens, loyal to the holy emperor. Accordingly, he convened in Constantinople in 443 AD a synod that passed a papal edict rejecting Origenism in general and reincarnation in particular.

3. Initially, Pope Vigilius opposed the imperial edict, even breaking off communication with the Emperor who had issued it. But when he arrived in Constantinople he reversed himself. To avoid the impression that the emperor had a say in matters of theology, he issued a separate document condemning the writings that the imperial edict had rejected.

4. The Pope's document was severely criticised by bishops in Gaul, North Africa and elsewhere and consequently, Vigilius withdrew it in 550 AD.

5. In 553 AD Justinian convened the whole Church in the Second Council of Constantinople—also known as the Fifth Ecumenical Council of the Church—in which the Church Fathers supporting Origenism were mostly not present. By thus stacking the votes against Origenism, he had his decree against Origenism handed down as a Papal Edict: "If anyone asserts the fabulous pre-existence of souls and the monstrous restoration which follows from it, let him be anathema (cursed)."

6. The Pope had completely opposed the emperor's convening this council and was not even present at this historic meeting. He tried to resist the Emperor by hiding from May to December. But on 23 February

554 he surrendered and officially ratified the council's condemnation of Origenism.

7. The churches in the West rebelled with some dioceses, closing communication with Rome until the seventh century. In Africa, the acceptance of the edicts had to be imposed by imperial troops.

Due to the questionable nature of the ecclesiastical proceedings and the complex web of theo-politics surrounding them, several modern Christian scholars (a) doubt whether the anathemas laid down by that particular Council are actually binding on Catholics, or (b) believe that Origen was never actually condemned by the Church, or (c) assume his condemnation was revoked and that modern Christians may thus adopt his reincarnationist teachings. Such reservations are elaborately described in a source as reliable as *The Catholic Encyclopaedia*.

Consequently, many Christian scholars consider the edict against reincarnation controversial and controvertible. For example, the globally renowned Swiss Catholic thinker Hans Kung, in his book *Eternal Life?: Life After Death as a Medical, Philosophical, and Theological Problem* advocates that Christianity should not only accept reincarnation but also elevate it to a central issue.

Other contemporary writers who accept reincarnation in the Christian tradition include John J. Hearney, Professor of Theology at Fordham University; William L. de Arteaga, a Christian minister; John H. Hick, Danforth Professor of Philosophy and Religion; and Quincy Howe, Jr., an Associate Professor of Classics at Scripps College and a graduate of Harvard, Columbia, and Princeton.

ISLAM

Like the scriptures of the other Abrahamic religions, the Koran too is relatively silent on reincarnation. Nonetheless, several Koranic verses hint at reincarnation. For example, the Koran (22.66) says: "He is the one who gave you life (*ahyakum*), then He will cause you to die (*yumitukum*), then He will give you life (*yuhyakum*) [again]." This same theme is repeated later in the Koran, as a warning for idol worshippers: "It is God who created you (*khalaqakum*), then provided for you, then He will cause you to die (*yumitukum*), then He will give you life (*yuhyikum*) [again]."

While these verses are presently taken to refer to resurrection, they can equally be taken to refer to reincarnation.

The renowned Islamic scholar G.F. Moore states in his Ingersoll lecture on transmigration that "among Mohammedans the difficulty of reconciling the sufferings of innocent children . . . with the goodness or even the justice of God led some of the liberal theologians (Mu'tazilites) to seek a solution in sins committed in a former existence . . . Reincarnation is fundamental to the doctrine of Imam as held by the [Shi'ites]; it was developed in a characteristic form by the Ism'ilis, and is a cardinal doctrine of Babism."

Islamic historian E.G. Browne elaborates these ideas in his classic three-volume work, *The Literary History of Persia*. While discussing the more esoteric schools of Islam he outlines three forms of transmigration accepted by classical Muslim thinkers: (1) *Hutul*, the periodical incarnation of a saint or prophet; (2) *Rij'at*, the immediate return of an Imam or any other important spiritual leader after death; and (3) *Tanasukh*, the ordinary reincarnation of all souls.

Sufism represents Islam's mystical side. Several Sufi saints have embraced reincarnation wholeheartedly. Typical of their beliefs is the following expression of Persian Muslim theologian and Sufi mystic Jalalu' I-din Rumi (1207-1273), "I died as mineral and became a plant, I died as a plant and rose to animal, I died as animal and I was Man. Why should I fear? When was I less by dying?"

Among the various groups within Islam, the Druze, who were known as the Sufis of Syria accept reincarnation as a foundational principle. Though this syncretic offshoot of Islam is considered heretical, this thousand-year-old tradition has steady followers in Lebanon, Jordan, and Syria.

To conclude, it is fitting to refer to the masterpiece of Islamic scholar Nadarbeg K. Mirza, *Reincarnation in Islam*, wherein he presents persuasive arguments establishing the compatibility of belief in reincarnation with the Koran in specific and the Islamic tradition in general.

BUDDHISM

Reincarnation is central to the teachings of Buddha and to Buddhist thought in general. This can be seen most vividly in the *Jataka Tales* ("Birth Stories"), which are 547 stories of the Buddha's past incarnations, many of which are said to have been told by the Buddha himself. These tales illustrate the compassion of Buddha by describing how he incarnated as a god, an animal, and even as a tree in order to help souls in various states of bondage to attain liberation. For example, one tale narrates how he incarnated as an elephant and helped a woman in distress by making immense sacrifices, even filing off his tusks for her sake. In her next life, that woman, recollecting his selfless sacrificing spirit, became his disciple and went on to become a great saint.

The cardinality of reincarnation in Buddhism is also evident in the process of determining the right successor for the post of the Dalai Lama, the spiritual head of Tibetan Buddhism. Traditionally, it is believed that whenever the reigning Dalai Lama dies he immediately takes birth again to continue his compassionate mission. Consequently, an extensive search is launched for the reborn Lama among children born at that time. The elaborate search process involves looking for both normal and mystical identification marks. Once the reincarnated Lama is identified, he is trained and groomed to become the successor.

Even in forms of Buddhism like Zen Buddhism that focus more on complex meditational techniques than on metaphysical questions, many Zen masters have expounded on reincarnation. For example, the great Zen master Chao-chou (778 – 897) taught, "Before the existence of the world, the Self-nature is. After the destruction of the world, the Self-nature remains intact." (Quoted in *The Golden Age of Zen* by John C. H. Wu)

While reincarnation has always been central to Buddhism, the existence of the soul has been disputed. Many schools of Buddhism today advocate a no-soul doctrine, claiming that there is no soul or any such distinct entity. Naturally, this raises the obvious question: who or what is it that moves from one body to the next? This question has caused considerable difficulty to Buddhist thinkers throughout its history.

Interestingly, there is a significant body of scholarship that states the no-soul doctrine didn't originate from the Buddha himself. For example, German *bhikku* George Grimm in his book *The Doctrine of the Buddha* reports the Buddha's reaction to the no-soul doctrine: "And I, O monks, am accused wrongly, vainly, falsely, and inappropriately, by some ascetics and *Brahmanas*: 'A denier is the ascetic Gotama, he teaches the destruction, annihilation, and perishing of the being that now exists.' These ascetics accuse me of being what I am not, O monks, and of saying what I do not say." Some scholars hold that the no-soul doctrine was a post-Buddha teaching appended by those who sought to assert Buddhism's ideological autonomy from Hinduism, which accepted the soul.

Thus, it can be concluded that the soul's eternality is, at the very least, compatible with Buddhism and that reincarnation is pivotal to Buddhism.

CHAPTER SEVEN

SOUL-SEARCHING— THE VEDIC WAY

*"Whenever I have read any part of the Vedas, I have felt that
some unearthly and unknown light illuminated me. In the
great teaching of the Vedas, there is no touch of sectarianism.
It is of all ages, climbs, and nationalities and is the royal road
for the attainment of the Great Knowledge."*
—American Thinker Henry David Thoreau

In the previous chapter, we discussed how the principle
of reincarnation has enjoyed acceptability and even
respectability nearly all over the world throughout
most of human history.

Once we have become aware of the prevalence of
reincarnation, we may naturally wonder, "How can we
know more about it? Where can we get systematic and
comprehensive knowledge about it?"

American author William Walker Atkinson,
pioneer of the New Thought Movement, in his book
Reincarnation and the Law of Karma, offers this answer:
"While reincarnation has been believed and taught in
nearly every nation, and among all races, in former or

present times, still we are justified in considering India as the natural Mother of the doctrine, inasmuch as it has found an especially favourable spiritual and mental environment in that land and among its people . . . The tree of the teaching being still in full flower and still bearing an abundance of fruit."

The Vedic literatures of ancient India and the wisdom-tradition that has grown around them do indeed offer a systematic and extensive explanation of reincarnation and the entity that reincarnates, the soul. Therefore, we will draw from this wisdom-tradition in this and the next chapter to unravel the mystery of reincarnation.

Some of us may hesitate to draw from ancient literatures during our present scientific age. However, benefitting from the insights of the past is a time-honoured tradition all over the world even within the world of science. The tradition of learning from the past is acknowledged and recommended by an authority no less than Isaac Newton, who remarked about his own contributions: "If I have seen further than others, it is by standing upon the shoulders of giants."

In chapters 1 to 4, we discussed various empirical pointers that make the principle of reincarnation scientifically at least tenable if not undeniable. Might the Vedic literature expand the boundaries of our understanding of the soul? Many eminent scientists including several Nobel Laureates have acknowledged that the insights from the Vedic literature may illumine the issues confronting modern science. Let's look at the quotes of two Nobel Laureates:

"After the conversations about Indian philosophy, some of
the ideas of quantum physics that had seemed so
crazy suddenly made much more sense."
–Nobel Laureate W. Heisenberg
(German Physicist, 1901 – 1976).

"The Vedanta and the Sankhya hold the key to the laws
of mind and thought process which are co-related to the
Quantum Field, i.e. the operation and distribution of
particles at atomic and molecular levels."
–Nobel Laureate Prof. Brian David Josephson (1940-),
the world's youngest Nobel Laureate.

The Vedic wisdom-tradition offers us a coherent, cogent, and
extensive body of knowledge about reincarnation. This body
of knowledge includes a vast galaxy of books that deal with the
soul and its reincarnation.

One of the best known and the most respected books
within the Vedic library is the philosophical classic, the
Bhagavad-gita. The wisdom of the *Bhagavad-gita* has been
appreciated by eminent thinkers all over the world including
scientists like Albert Einstein and Robert Oppenheimer;
philosophers like Ralph Waldo Emerson, Henry David
Thoreau, Rudolph Steiner, and Albert Schweitzer; apostles
of peace like Mohandas Gandhi; and literary luminaries like
Herman Hesse and Aldous Huxley. For example, Huxley
underscores the universality of the *Bhagavad-gita*: "The
Bhagavad-gita is the most systematic statement of spiritual
evolution of endowing value to mankind. It is one of the most
clear and comprehensive summaries of perennial philosophy

ever revealed; hence its enduring value is subject not only to India but to all of humanity."

Central to this wisdom-tradition's explanation of reincarnation is the concept of the soul, the entity that transmigrates from one body to the next. While the concept of the soul is mentioned in most ancient wisdom-traditions, it is clearly and analytically explained in the Vedic wisdom-tradition in general and the *Bhagavad-gita* in particular. This tradition treats the soul not vaguely as a metaphorical reference to our intangible essence but concretely as a very real spiritual entity with its own distinctive characteristics.

CHARACTERISTICS OF THE SOUL

Let's discuss these characteristics of the soul one-by-one.

1. **The Soul Is the Source of Consciousness in the Body**
   In the fifth chapter of this book, we have discussed how consciousness does not originate in the brain. Then where does it originate? The *Bhagavad-gita* explains that it originates in the soul. The *Bhagavad-gita* (13.34) illustrates the relationship between the soul and consciousness with a vivid example: "As the sun alone illuminates all this universe, so does the living entity, one within the body, illuminate the entire body by consciousness."

   This implies that just as sunlight is the symptom of the sun, consciousness is the symptom of the soul. If we are inside a room and can't see the sun in the sky outside, we can still infer its presence by observing its symptom: sunlight. Similarly, even if we can't see the soul inside the body, we can still infer its presence by observing its symptom: consciousness.

Another more contemporary metaphor to illustrate the soul-body relationship is the driver-car relationship. Just as the driver is the cause of the motion of the car, the soul is the cause of activity and other symptoms of consciousness seen in the body. Even when the car has the full mechanical, functional capacity to move, it cannot move by itself without activation by the driver. Similarly, even when the body has the full biochemical functional capacity to act, it cannot act by itself without activation of some sort by the soul.

2. The Soul Is Unaffected by Anything Material

The *Bhagavad-gita* (2.23) states, "The soul can never be cut to pieces by any weapon, nor burned by fire, nor moistened by water, nor withered by the wind."

In this verse, the *Bhagavad-gita* gives us a vivid sense of the spiritual nature of the soul. The statement that the soul is not affected by the various common agents that affect the material body, viz., weapons, fire, water, and wind conveys an understanding of what it means for the soul to be beyond matter.

3. The Soul Is Indestructible

The *Bhagavad-gita* (2.17) states, "That which pervades the entire body you should know to be indestructible. No one is able to destroy that imperishable soul."

Thus, the soul is eternal and is not subject to the destruction that is inevitable for the material body. Even after the body is destroyed the soul lives on and on, forever.

4. The Soul Is Entirely Different from the Material Body

The *Bhagavad-gita* (2.22) states, "As a person puts on new garments, giving up old ones, the soul similarly accepts new material bodies, giving up the old and useless ones."

By comparing the material body with a dress that is periodically discarded and replaced, the *Bhagavad-gita* highlights the temporary nature of the relationship between the body and the soul. The impermanence of this relationship underscores that the body and the soul are fundamentally and categorically different. This radical difference between the body and the soul makes possible the soul's transfer from one material body to an entirely different material body, a transfer essential for reincarnation.

5. The Soul Is Extremely Small

The size of the soul is indicated in another important book in the Vedic wisdom-tradition, the *Shvetashvatara Upanishad* (5.9): "When the upper point of the hair is divided into hundred parts and each of such part is further divided into hundred parts, each such part is the measurement of the dimension of the spirit soul."

In other words, the soul is extremely minute in size. So let us reflect for a moment: who exactly are we? We are the eternal spirit soul, one ten-thousandth of a tip of a strand of hair. Isn't that a humbling thought?

6. The Soul Is an Individual Eternally

"Never was there a time when I [Krishna] did not exist,

nor you, nor all these kings; nor in the future shall any of us cease to be." (*Bhagavad-gita* 2.12)

This verse asserts that individuality is an eternal feature of all living beings. Is this eternal individuality a feature of the body or of the soul? It cannot be a feature of the body because the body is perishable. Therefore, eternal individuality is a feature of the soul; as souls, we remain individuals forever even though the bodies we occupy perish one after another.

7. The Soul Is Amazing

"Some look on the soul as amazing, some describe it as amazing, and some hear of it as amazing, while others, even after hearing about it, cannot understand it at all."(*Bhagavad-gita* 2.29)

Why is the soul described as amazing? One reason is the mind-boggling variety of the bodily habitats that it can enliven. Bhaktivedanta Swami, a prominent modern exponent of the *Gita*, explains, "The fact that the atomic soul is within the body of a gigantic animal, in the body of a gigantic banyan tree, and also in the microbic germs, millions of which occupy only an inch of space, is certainly very amazing."

8. The Soul Is Situated in the Region of the Heart

The *Mundaka Upanishad* (3.1.9) states, "The soul is atomic in size and can be perceived by perfect intelligence. This atomic soul is situated in the region of the heart, and spreads its influence all over the body of the embodied living entity."

We may wonder what happens to the soul when the heart is transplanted. The heart is the seat for the soul just as the throne is the seat for the king. When an old throne is replaced with a new throne, the king doesn't get replaced but just shifts to the new throne. Similarly, when an old heart needs to be replaced with a new heart, the soul doesn't get replaced but just shifts to the new heart.

TWO KINDS OF BODIES

The Vedic wisdom-tradition explains that the soul is covered by two kinds of bodies (see the diagram below):

1. **The Gross Material Body** is the visible body that we feed and dress and normally identify ourselves with.
2. **The Subtle Material Body** is the mechanism that serves as an interface between the soul and the gross material body. It comprises of the mind, the intelligence, and the false ego.

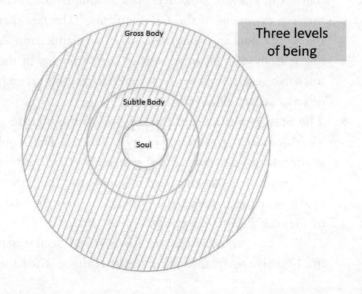

Gross Body

Three levels of being

Subtle Body

Soul

Pertinent to note is the difference between the soul and the mind: the soul is the *root* of consciousness, whereas the mind is a *route* of consciousness. The mind is the medium through which the soul interacts with the body and the world outside. The soul is conscious whereas the mind being material is not. The mind merely reflects the consciousness of the soul.

Significantly, just as the gross body has gross senses the subtle body has subtle senses. Thus, for example, just as the gross body has a physical eye, the subtle body has a subtle eye; and just as the gross body has a physical ear, the subtle body has a subtle ear.

To better understand how the soul functions through the gross and subtle bodies, let's consider an intriguing metaphor described in an important philosophical treatise in the Vedic library, the *Katha Upanishad* (1.3.3-4): "The soul is the passenger in the chariot of the material body, and intelligence is the charioteer. The mind is the reins, and the senses are the horses. The self is thus the enjoyer or sufferer in the association of the mind and senses. So it is understood by great thinkers."

Just as the unrestrained horses pull the reins in the different directions in which they feel tempted, the unrestrained senses pull the mind toward the various attractive worldly objects that they encounter. The *Bhagavad-gita* (15.9) indicates that the mind is the centre that integrates the impressions coming from the senses. These impressions generally tend to agitate the mind. Just as the charioteer uses the reins to restrain the horses, the intelligence uses the mind to restrain the senses.

Further, the chariot metaphor also illustrates how the subtle body serves as a link between the soul and the gross body. Just as the passenger directs the horses through the charioteer and the reins, the soul directs the gross body through the subtle body comprising the intelligence and the mind.

THE MODEL'S EXPLANATORY POTENTIAL

Let's now see how this Vedic model of consciousness can help explain baffling phenomena, such as near-death experiences, and past-life memories.

1. **Near-Death Experiences**

   As discussed in the fourth chapter of this book, several near-death experiencers have reported accurate perceptions from an out-of-body perspective during conditions of documented medical unconsciousness. Such perceptions are unexplainable with the materialist model of the self.

   Let's see whether the Vedic model can help us arrive at an answer.

   In the Vedic model the soul's consciousness is usually transmitted through the subtle body to the brain and then from the brain to the external world.

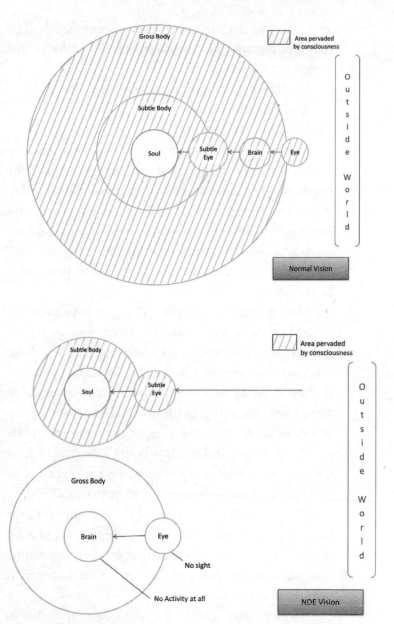

Let's consider the act of seeing as an example. The soul sees the outside world through the pathway that comprises:

1. The subtle body, especially the subtle eye,
2. The visual areas of the brain, and
3. The physical eyes.

When a person is unconscious, this normal pathway is obstructed as the physical eyes are closed and the visual areas of the brain are dysfunctional. Nonetheless, the soul remains conscious and the subtle sense of sight remains capable of functioning. Therefore, even during medical unconsciousness the patient can see with the subtle eye if the obstacle on the visual pathway is bypassed.

How might this happen? It might happen if the soul, along with the subtle body, comes out of the gross body. The soul might exit thus under those special circumstances when the body is damaged and dysfunctional as in some near-death experiences. In these cases, the soul can observe the gross body from an out-of-body overhead perspective using the subtle eye that is a part of the subtle body. This may be how near-death experiencers can perceive even when their body and brain are documented to be unconscious.

Thus, the Vedic model can account for the factual perceptions during near-death experiences. Additionally, it can explain an even more intriguing phenomenon: the ability of the blind to see during their near-death experiences.

As mentioned earlier, Kenneth Ring and Sharon

Cooper in their book *Mindsight: Near-Death and Out-of-Body Experiences in the Blind* have documented several cases of verified visual perceptions by blind people during their near-death experiences. In these individuals, their bodily channel of sight had been irreparably damaged, rendering them incapable of seeing anything. If the capacity of sight were originating in and dependent exclusively on the bodily parts associated with seeing, then these people should never have been able to see anything. Yet during their NDEs they were able to see, though they weren't able to see anything before or after.

Key to understanding their NDE vision is the differentiation in the Vedic model between the sensory organs in the gross material body and the subtle senses in the subtle material body. Normally, any physical damage in the visual pathway obstructs the soul's seeing capacity. But during the NDE, when the soul and the subtle body are separated from the gross body, then the physical damage no longer blocks the soul's path of sight. And the soul can see using the sense of sight provided by the subtle body. After the NDE, when the soul returns to the body, the normal physical blockage again prevents the person from seeing.

2. **Past-Life Memories**

In the first three chapters of this book, we discussed that many children in various parts of the world remember precise details about deceased persons, who they claim to have been in a previous life. What makes these cases especially mysterious is that the children could not have known these precise details by any normal means.

Let's see how the Vedic model explains such past-life memories.

At the moment of death, the soul along with the subtle body leaves the gross body, and moves to another gross body. The Vedic model explains that our memories are stored not just in the physical brain but also in the subtle mind from which they can be accessed by the brain whenever needed. (Incidentally, this non-cerebral storage of memories can also explain how our memories endure even when our brain cells change and are replaced—an enigma that we discussed in chapter five.)

As the subtle body moves along with the soul after death to the next body, the memories of the previous life are hypothetically available for the soul to recall in the next life. Normally however, the trauma caused by the momentous transitions of death and birth buries these memories so deep within the mind that, for most of us, they don't seem to exist at all.

Forgetfulness of our past lives enables us to start a new life afresh without being burdened by the memories of the past. This burden can be agonizing and disorienting: agonizing because of the many traumatic memories involved; and disorienting because it would make living according to our present bodily identity difficult.

Nonetheless, some individuals can, under certain special circumstances recollect some details of their previous lives. Often, the memories of the past lives occur among individuals who died in ways that were sudden, or violent, or both. The abrupt nature of their death may not allow them to process the event of death properly; so when they acquire their next body the unprocessed memories of the event remain as a sort of hangover.

Another mysterious feature of past-life memories cases is that some children have birthmarks and birth defects at the same precise locations where the person they remember being had fatal wounds or other distinct bodily marks. How might this happen? Many scientifically documented reports have shown that mental impressions can express themselves as bodily marks. Ian Stevenson presents an overview of these reports in a chapter entitled *Bodily Changes Corresponding to Mental Images in the Person Affected* in his book *Where Reincarnation and Biology Intersect*. The Vedic model can help us understand how the same principle can be extended from the body of one lifetime to the body of the next lifetime.

As explained earlier, during reincarnation the mind that is the bearer of mental impressions goes along with the soul from the previous gross body to the next gross body. So when the previous gross body was inflicted with the fatal wounds, the impressions of that wound were created on the mind. And when that mind along with the soul enters into the next body, it causes those impressions to get expressed as birthmarks or birth defects at the corresponding bodily locations.

After thus seeing how the Vedic model explains NDEs and past-life memories, let us now go deeper into this model.

INTUITING THE SOUL'S ESSENTIAL NATURE

We can intuit the soul's essential nature as well as its presence in various living beings through sustained reflection. Vedic wisdom states that the soul is, by its very nature, *sac-cid-ananda*: eternal, full of knowledge, and full of bliss. Is this eternal, enlightened, and ecstatic nature of the soul expressed in any way in our present bodily existence? Let's analyse these three aspects of our nature.

Eternality

Normally, all of us long to live forever; we can hardly consider the prospect of a future in which we won't have any part to play, in which we won't exist at all. We instinctively recoil at the thought of our own mortality, and in this, we are not alone. Even the tiniest of creatures displays the most amazing skills to avoid death.

This universal longing for life is all the more remarkable when contrasted with the verity that death is the most unchangeable and undeniable of all facts of life. All physical bodies are doomed to mortality; they are born with a death sentence, an expiry date written on them.

If we are just our physical bodies, then why do we have such a deep-rooted desire for something—eternal existence—that is so utterly unnatural, even impossible, for the physical body to attain? How does this deep-rooted longing originate in a world that demonstrates its inevitable frustration ubiquitously, in our own and others' dying bodies? The Vedic wisdom-tradition answers that this longing comes from the innermost essence of our being, the soul, which is by nature eternal. We long to live forever because we, as souls, are eternal.

Cognizance

All of us are insatiably curious. Some people are curious about the latest celebrity gossip; others, about the breaking global news; still others, about the nature of the furthest stars. Though what we want to know varies from person to person, the principle of wanting to know more remains common to all.

Again, we humans are not alone in being actuated by a curiosity drive; experiments have shown that monkeys work longer and harder to discover what lies on the other side of a trapdoor than to get food or sex. If we try to understand this curiosity drive in the context of the notion that we are just our physical bodies, we encounter a logical dead end. Our physical bodies allow us only a few small windows to the outer world. Through these windows called senses, we can know only very little of what exists and occurs there. No doubt, we have learnt quite a bit about the world using our mind and senses. But the very expansion of our learning has expanded our vision of how much more there is to be learnt.

Our hi-tech probes have helped us learn something about atoms—and have also revealed how complex the atom actually is. This has brought into sharper focus not just how little we know but how little we can know. If we are just our physical bodies, then why do we have a hunger for knowledge that we are physically so incapable of satisfying? From the Vedic perspective, our insatiable curiosity originates in the soul, which is by nature conscious and knowledgeable.

Blissfulness

All of us are instinctively happiness-seeking. Be it through indulging in sensual pleasures, performing heroic feats, participating in life-risking sports, watching TV soap operas, reading literature, hearing music, or playing video games, pleasure is what we constantly seek. Again, studies of the behaviour of animals have shown that they too strive for pleasure. Yet the physical body allows us very few avenues for pleasure; these avenues are limited to the contact points of the senses and the things that give them pleasure. And the same body can cause us pain through practically each one of its organs. The number of bodily pleasures are few; the number of bodily diseases and distresses, numerous.

Indeed, the ways in which the body can inflict pain far outnumber the ways in which it can yield pleasure. If we were just our material bodies, then why would we have a thirst for pleasure that we are physically so ill-equipped to quench? The Vedic wisdom-tradition responds that our thirst for pleasure originates in the joyfulness that is inherent to the soul.

Thus, by soberly reflecting on the contrasting natures of our innate longings and our bodily trappings, we can glimpse the nature of the soul.

Some of us may wonder, "If I am actually immortal, then why don't I *feel* indestructible? Why do I feel so susceptible to destruction?"

The answer, the Vedic wisdom-tradition says, lies in the depth at which the soul is buried beneath a nearly impenetrable mass of misconceived notions and misdirected cravings. Our past prolonged actions under a materialistic conception of life have created deep impressions on our psyche that have almost entirely obscured our awareness of our spiritual identity.

TWO CONCEPTIONS, TWO CONCLUSIONS

Let's now look at a classic Vedic story that illustrates this dynamic project of spiritual excavation through introspection and purification.

The *Chandogya Upanishad* (8.7 – 8.12), an ancient Vedic text, narrates the story of two individuals who sought to know the true nature of the self: Indra, the king of the godly beings, and Virocana, the king of the ungodly beings.

Brahma, the creator, famed for his deep spiritual wisdom, desired to benefit all living beings. So he proclaimed the importance of knowledge of the self, "The self is free from sin, old age, death, grief, hunger, and thirst. All need to search out and understand this self, for then we will attain complete fulfilment."

Hearing Brahma's proclamation, Indra and Virocana approached him to acquire that knowledge of the self. Accepting him as their spiritual mentor, they adopted a lifestyle of discipline and austerity. After they had purified themselves for thirty-two years, they requested Brahma for more insight. Brahma responded, "The person that you see with the eyes is the self; that soul is fearless and immortal."

To verify their understanding, Indra and Virocana asked, "The reflection we see before our eyes in a river or a mirror—is that the soul?"

Nodding, Brahma replied, "Look at yourself in a pan of water, and report to me what you see there."

After looking, they informed Brahma, "We see the complete self, from the hair on top of our heads to the toenails on our feet."

Then, Brahma asked them to trim their hair and toenails and to adorn themselves with new clothes and ornaments.

When they did so, he asked them, "What do you see now?" They replied, "The two persons in these reflections have cut their hair and toenails, just as we have. And they are dressed in new clothes and adorned with ornaments, just as we are."

Brahma told them, "What you see in the reflection is the fearless and immortal soul."

Indra and Virocana departed, delighted with their newfound knowledge.

Virocana returned to his people, the ungodly beings, and announced to them, "The body is nondifferent from the soul, so the body alone is to be worshipped, the body alone is to be served. He who does so gains both this world and the next."

Indra, however, became pensive. On the way back to his abode, he thought, "The reflection in the water changes when the body changes; when the body is cleaned, it becomes clean. So, when the body perishes, it will also perish. How, then, can it be the immortal soul?"

Thinking thus, Indra returned to Brahma, who asked him to stay and delve deeper into the truths of the self.

After Indra had performed another thirty-two years of austerities, Brahma told him, "The 'I' in your dreams is the self you are seeking. The person you understand to be the self in your dreams—that is the fearless and immortal soul."

Happy with this insight, Indra departed. But again, on his return journey he was overcome by doubt: "The self in my dreams sometimes feels fear and pain. The self of the dreams departs when the dream ends and so it is temporary. Moreover, that self is an imaginary, ever-changing entity – blind in one dream, multi-headed in another, and lame in yet another. How can it be the fearless, immortal soul?"

Troubled, Indra returned to Brahma, who urged him to study some more. After he performed austerity for another thirty-two years, Brahma told him, "The self lies hidden in the state of deep sleep that is entirely dreamless."

As before, Indra felt initially joyous, then dubious. He thought, "In deep sleep, the self does not perceive anything at all; he is not aware of anything in existence, not even his own self. It is as if the self is annihilated. This can't be the fearless, immortal self."

Indra submitted his doubt to Brahma. The preceptor nodded and told him to stay on a while longer.

After five more years of austerity, Brahma revealed the ultimate truth: "The physical body is just the abode for the true self, the soul, concealed within. Just as a horse is yoked to a cart, the soul is attached to the body. The body is forever subject to fear and death. When one breaks the attachment to the body, he realises the fearless and immortal soul. It is the soul who sees through the eyes, and hears through the ears. Beyond its present life of bodily attachment, the soul has its own life in relationship with God."

This story illustrates, through Indra's example, what is necessary for understanding one's true identity: unrelenting introspection that is not satisfied with shallow answers and unflinching purification that accepts whatever austerity is necessary to get to the truth. Those who are satisfied with superficial answers like Virocana get sidetracked.

Additionally the story illustrates the different levels at which we may misperceive our identity. The most common misperception, the one with which both Indra and Virocana started and the one which Virocana never relinquished, is misidentification with the gross physical body.

For those who go beyond this misperception, the next level of misidentification is with the subtle body, where one identifies with one's thoughts. Sometimes, as in this story, this level is divided into two states of covered consciousness. Those who probe further and enquire who is thinking the thoughts get the full insight: they realise their true identity as souls beyond coverings, physical and mental.

THE HOME TERRITORY OF CONSCIOUSNESS

The levels of misidentification in this story also correspond with the different operational levels of consciousness explained in the Vedic wisdom-tradition. The *Bhagavata Purana* (7.7.25) mentions these three levels to be *jagruti* (waking consciousness), *svapna* (dreaming consciousness), and *sushupti* (dreamless sleeping consciousness). Beyond these three is the original consciousness of the soul, which is called *turiya* (spiritually wakeful consciousness).

Let's take a closer look at these four states based on the explanation given in another Vedic text, the *Mandukya Upanishad* (mantras 3 – 7):

Waking consciousness

At this operational level of consciousness, we are aware of the physical world around us; the consciousness originating from the soul is routed through the subtle body and the gross body to the outer world. At this level, we generally misidentify ourselves with our gross physical body. This was the level at which both Indra and Virocana started.

Dreaming consciousness

This operational level of consciousness is characterised by the presence of mental activity and the suspension of sense activity. The consciousness from the soul is extended primarily until the subtle body. As consciousness is essential for perception and action, this level is characterised by perception and action at the mental level, but not at the physical level. At this level, we misidentify with the mind, as indicated in the second answer given by Brahma.

Dreamless sleeping consciousness

At this level, there is suspension of mental activity and the absence of even dreams, so there is no awareness of anything at all, as indicated in Brahma's third answer. Consciousness is not routed even to the subtle body at this level.

Sometimes doctors classify patients as "unconscious" or even "comatose," and use, say, the Glasgow Coma Scale to measure the depth of the coma. Even in such cases, the Vedic wisdom-tradition asserts that consciousness, being an inalienable characteristic of the soul is still present; it is just not being expressed at the physical or mental levels. Put succinctly, unconsciousness is also a state of consciousness.

Spiritually wakeful consciousness

This is the original, natural level of consciousness in which the soul is in home territory, perceiving its own spiritual identity as well as the spiritual realm. This is the level that Indra finally glimpsed through sustained introspection and purification.

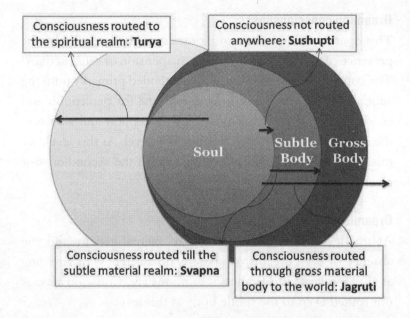

Consciousness routed to the spiritual realm: **Turya**

Consciousness not routed anywhere: **Sushupti**

Soul

Subtle Body

Gross Body

Consciousness routed till the subtle material realm: **Svapna**

Consciousness routed through gross material body to the world: **Jagruti**

REALISATION THROUGH DEVOTIONAL CONNECTION

By similar introspection and purification, we too may be able to realise our nature as souls. But it is a dreary, dicey, and drawn-out process; Indra needed over a hundred years of exhaustive and exclusive practice.

Some of us may wonder why Brahma didn't give the real answer straight away. His strategy is in harmony with the overall purpose of the *Upanishads*. These complex metaphysical literatures comprise the *jnana-kanda* section of the Vedic literature, which offers spiritual insight custom-made for those who delight in their own intellectual prowess. Accordingly, it employs a strategy technically called *neti-neti* (not this, not this), a strategy that focuses on negation of misconceptions and a subtle, gradual, progressive affirmation of the correct conception.

The *Bhagavad-gita* embodies the essential wisdom of the *Upanishads,* just as milk embodies the essential gift of a cow. So the *Gita* conveys clearly and directly the teachings that are conveyed obscurely and indirectly in the *Upanishads.*

When we thus guide our consciousness inwards through introspection and purification, we will realise the mysterious soul and discover that the investigator of the mystery was the goal of the mystery: I, the seeker of the soul, am myself the soul.

CHAPTER EIGHT

REINCARNATION—THE HOWS AND THE WHYS

"Has it occurred to you that transmigration is at once an explanation and a justification of the evil of the world? If the evils we suffer are the result of sins committed in our past lives, we can bear them with resignation and hope that if in this one we strive towards virtue, our future lives will be less afflicted."

—W. Somerset Maugham in The Razor's Edge

The reflective understanding of our spiritual identity is best possible for humans, who alone have the capacity for metaphysical enquiry. In fact, this potential for spiritual realisation is the characteristic that fundamentally distinguishes humans from animals— as is acknowledged by the world's great spiritual traditions, whether Western or Eastern.

DO ANIMALS HAVE SOULS?

From the universal fact of human specialness, some people make the sectarian extrapolation that humans alone have souls and animals don't. They feel that our human consciousness with its potential for spirituality is too distinctive and too irreducible to be equated with the level of consciousness of beasts. Beasts, according to this line of thought, don't have souls—or at least not souls of the same kind that we humans have.

From the Vedic perspective, this idea confuses our humanity with our spirituality; it attributes to our human body the spiritual characteristics that belong to our soul.

The Vedic wisdom-tradition declares that souls are present in all living beings, whether human or animal. Moreover, the tradition also emphasises that all souls present in all these living beings are essentially of the same kind; they all have the same nature of being eternal-cognizant-ecstatic (*sat-cit-anand*).

The existence of souls in animals can be inferred from the general observation that animals exhibit the same symptoms of life that we humans do. Animals engage in the same array of activities as humans: eating, sleeping, mating, defending, and so on. The main difference is humans, being endowed with a higher intellect, can do these activities in more sophisticated ways than animals can.

The presence of the soul is also evident through the remarkable difference in the behaviour of living organisms and non-living systems. Non-living systems have three phases to their existence: creation, deterioration, and destruction. Living organisms exhibit three more phases: growth, reproduction, and maintenance. These additional phases, the Vedic texts explain, are due to the presence of the soul. And as these six changes are exhibited not just by humans but also by animals, we can safely infer that animals too have souls.

The unique human capacity for metaphysical enquiry is not simply because humans have souls but because the human body covers the consciousness of the soul, less than an animal body does. The *Bhagavad-gita* (3.38) states: "As fire is covered by smoke, as a mirror is covered by dust, or as the embryo is covered by the womb, the living entity is similarly covered to different degrees."

In this metaphor-rich verse, the smoke-covered fire refers to the soul covered by a human body, the dust-covered mirror refers to the soul covered by an animal body, and the womb-covered embryo refers to the soul covered by a plant body. The coverings become increasingly thick from smoke through dust to embryo. Similarly, the covering on the soul becomes increasingly thick from the human body through the animal body to the plant body. As this covering is least in the human body, humans can express the soul's spirituality to the greatest degree. Thus, the difference between humans and animals is not a difference of nature, but of degree; not a difference in essential nature but a difference in the degree of expression of the soul's consciousness.

BREAKING FREE FROM ANTHROPOCENTRISM

The idea that only humans have souls is not only dubious in its content but also deleterious in its consequence. This idea fosters an anthropocentrism or human-centeredness that de-spiritualises animals and reduces the entire animal world to an inconsequential backdrop in the whole sphere of existence.

Such a human-centred view can breed the idea that the existence of animals has no intrinsic value; their only value is in the ways in which they are of use to us humans. Once animals have been thus de-spiritualised and devalued, they can easily be objectified. Such an objectified view of animals often paves the way to the proliferation of thousands of factory farms that treat animals as worse than soul-less creatures. These farms view animals as insentient commercial objects, whose only value is as factors in our economic equations as bearers of a price tag.

The idea that humans alone have souls can de-spiritualise not just the animal world but also all life forms, and indeed the totality of our environment. Underlying this is the notion that humans are the centre of all existence, that everything in nature is meant for human use alone. Such anthropocentrism naturally breeds the arrogant and exploitative mentality that is a primary cause of many of the ills of the modern world such as the environmental crisis.

In heartening contrast to this heartless view of the world around us, the Vedic worldview recognises and respects the intrinsic value of every living being. It rejects the anthropocentrism that makes the soul a monopoly of humans. By thus breaking free of anthropocentrism, the Vedic worldview integrates all living beings within a progression of spiritual evolution. No living being lives in vain, to struggle fitfully for life, only to die futilely and be obliterated forever out of existence. Every living being, no matter how insignificant its life may seem from our perspective is through its existence taking small yet significant steps onwards in its progressive spiritual evolution.

THE MECHANISM OF REINCARNATION

What happens to the soul after death? All of us have faced this question at some time or the other. Many people shrug off the question as unanswerable.

The Vedic wisdom-tradition answers this profound question by systematically delineating the broad principles that shape the soul's post-mortem journey.

Firstly, the tradition underscores the universality of reincarnation: it is not an exotic occurrence reserved for a privileged few but an impartial natural phenomenon that applies to all living beings. As the soul is eternal, when it leaves one body, it has to sooner or later acquire another body. Thus, reincarnation is not a sectarian Eastern notion but is an inherent feature of nature itself.

The soul's post-mortem journey can be divided into three broad successive stages:

1. The soul's exit from the present body,
2. Its travel to the location of its next body, and
3. Its entry into that body.

Let's look at these three stages briefly one-by-one:

1. The Soul's Exit from the Body

The Vedic wisdom-tradition explains that death occurs when the soul leaves the gross material body permanently. At the time of death, the soul normally exits from one of the nine holes in the body. These nine holes are the two eyes, the two ears, the two nostrils, the mouth, and the two excretory organs.

The *Brihadaranyaka Upanishad* (4.4.1-2) outlines this process of exit:

"[At the time of death] the area of his [the soul's] heart becomes lit and by that light the soul departs either through the eye, the head, or through other apertures of the body. And when he departs, the *pranas* [the various life airs] follow him to his next destination ... His knowledge and his deeds follow him, as does his previous wisdom, if not specific details of his former life."

Souls that are morally or spiritually evolved generally depart from the seven holes that lie on the upper side of the body, whereas other souls depart from the two lower holes. The location of the exit points through which a soul departs indicates its post-mortem destination. The souls who depart through the upper holes are headed towards the higher, more evolved realms of the universe whereas the souls who depart through the lower holes are headed toward the lower, less evolved realms of the universe.

When the soul exits from the gross body at the moment of death, it is accompanied by the subtle body. Normally, the soul is strongly attached to the body because of misidentifying with it. Due to this attachment, the soul feels its exit from the body agonising, just as a tenant feels eviction from his or her house agonising. Even after departing from the body, the soul being attached continues to hover around it with the hope of re-entering it. The Vedic tradition aids the soul in its onward journey by recommending the cremation of the dead body. When the soul sees the body irreversibly destroyed, having been reduced to a pile of ashes, the bonds that keep it close to the body are largely severed. Consequently, it becomes more ready to continue its journey to the next body.

2. The Soul's Journey to the Next Body

When the soul sets off on its journey to the next body, it is given a transitional body that is grosser than the subtle body and subtler than the gross body. Equipped with this body that is called in the Vedic literature as *preta*, the soul is taken by nature's arrangement to its post-mortem destination. The soul often finds this journey painful because its transitional body is highly susceptible to pain. To help ease the soul's pain, the Vedic literatures like the *Garuda Purana* recommend that the relatives of the deceased person perform certain activities whose merit cushions the soul's onward journey.

In exceptional cases when the soul does not get a next gross body, it stays in a disembodied state. Souls living this disembodied existence are called ghosts. Of course, ghosts are not entirely disembodied; they still have a subtle body. But because in general parlance the word "body" connotes a gross body, the state of existence without that body is called "disembodied." Those interested in knowing more about ghosts can refer to appendix 3 *Ghosts Demystified*.

3. The Soul's Entry into the Next Body

The *Bhagavata Purana* (3.31.1) outlines a typical pathway by which the soul enters into the next body: "The soul is made to enter into the womb of a woman through the particle of male semen to assume a particular type of body."

According to the Vedic wisdom-tradition, it is the presence of the soul that causes the zygote to grow into an infant and eventually into a grown-up person. The *Bhagavata Purana*, despite having been written thousands of years ago, gives a fascinating description of the growth of the infant in the womb, a description that matches remarkably with that found in standard texts of modern medical science. Here is a brief glimpse of the information given there:

"On the first night, the sperm and ovum mix, and on the fifth night the mixture ferments into a bubble. On the tenth night, it develops into a form like a plum, and after that it gradually turns into a lump of flesh. In the course of a month, a head is formed, and at the end of two months the hands, feet, and other limbs take shape. By the end of three months, the nails, fingers, toes, body hair, bones, and skin appear, as do the organ of generation and the other apertures in the body, namely the eyes, nostrils, ears, mouth and anus. Within four months from the date of conception, the seven essential ingredients of the body (lymph, blood, flesh, fat, bone, marrow, and semina) come into existence. At the end of five months, hunger and thirst make themselves felt, and at the end of six months, the foetus begins to move in the abdomen-on the right side if the child is a male and on the left side if female." (*Bhagavata Purana* 3.31.2-4)

This pre-natal description refers, of course, to a soul who has entered a human womb and is on course to getting a human body. However, all souls don't necessarily get human bodies in their next lives.

WHAT DETERMINES OUR NEXT BODY?

Which specific body a particular soul gets is determined by the broad principles that underlie the mechanism of reincarnation.

The *Brihadaranyaka Upanishad* (4.4.3-4) illustrates this mechanism with two graphic examples:

"Just as a caterpillar, when it reaches the end of one blade of grass, and after having properly approached another one, draws itself together toward the new blade, so the soul, after having thrown away the prior body and its ignorance, draws itself together, and latches onto the new body. And as the goldsmith, taking a piece of gold, turns it into another, more beautiful shape, even so does this soul, after having thrown away the old and useless body, makes unto himself newer and, hopefully, better bodies, according to his previous actions, ability and desires."

The *Bhagavad-gita* (15.8) also offers an additional example for the mechanism of reincarnation: just as the air carries aromas, the soul carries its different conceptions of life from one body to another.

Here's another helpful metaphor given in the *Bhagavad-gita* (2.22). The body is like a dress for the soul. Reincarnation therefore is akin to the shedding of an old dress and the acceptance of a new dress.

Just as our new dress is usually determined by our likes and our budget, the soul's new bodily dress is similarly determined by its desires and its karmic score. Let's take a closer look at these two factors.

Desires: The Vedic wisdom-tradition explains that the various species in nature act as variegated facilities for fulfilling the desires of the soul. For example, if a human being desires fervently to fly—or, more precisely, a soul in a human body desires fervently to fly—nature facilitates the fulfilment of that soul's desire by giving it the body of a bird.

Karmic score: Karma essentially implies that our actions have inbuilt consequences which we will have to bear in due course of time. Our karmic score refers to the sum of the consequences of all our actions. Those with a negative karmic score have done more actions that beget negative consequences than actions that beget positive consequences. Those with a positive karmic score have done more actions that beget positive consequences than actions that beget negative consequences. A negative karmic score gives the soul a less endowed body, a body lower down in the cosmic hierarchy of bodies. A positive karmic score gives the soul a more endowed body, a body higher up in the cosmic hierarchy of bodies.

Let's now look at this hierarchy.

UNDERSTANDING VEDIC TAXONOMY

Vedic taxonomy or system of classification begins by stating that all living beings belong to one of 8.4 million species. An important Vedic text, the *Padma Purana*, divides these 8.4 million species into six broad categories: 0.9 million species of aquatic life-forms, 2 million species of plants, 1.1 million species of insects and reptiles, 0.1 million species of birds, 3 million species of birds, and 0.4 million species of humans.

These 8.4 million species comprise a graded hierarchy with the aquatics and plants at the bottom and humans at the top. The bodies lower down in the hierarchy allow lesser expression of the soul's consciousness whereas the bodies higher up allow greater expression of the soul's consciousness.

This hierarchy also serves as the pathway for the soul's progressive reincarnation. Thus, for example, a soul in a plant body goes through multiple upward reincarnations automatically by nature's arrangement until it gets a human body. This progression of the soul through various species that allow more and more expression of its consciousness can be called the evolution of the soul or spiritual evolution.

In this spiritual evolution, humans are near the summit because the human body, as compared to all other bodies, allows the maximum expression of the soul's consciousness. More specifically the human body allows the soul the faculty to make metaphysical enquiry and to thereby realise its eternal nature.

Not all humans utilise the faculty for metaphysical enquiry because different humans are at different levels of consciousness. Taking this into account the Vedic wisdom-tradition doesn't place all humans in one species, as does modern biology. Instead, it asserts that humans according to their level of consciousness, can belong to any one of 0.4 million species, all of which are broadly subsumed in the species called humans. Clearly, Vedic taxonomy uses the word "species" differently from the way modern biology uses it. The perceptiveness of Vedic taxonomy is noteworthy: it considers not just the gross features like morphological characteristics of various living beings but also their subtle features like levels of consciousness.

CAN HUMANS REINCARNATE AS ANIMALS?

Some people who recognise that animals have souls still claim that the evolution of the soul is only upwards, never downwards.

They hold that once the soul attains a human body, it will never again fall back to the animal world.

It is true that the evolution of the soul through the lower sub-human species is usually upwards. But things change when the soul gets a human body. Why? Because the human body allows the soul to express its free will substantially. If the soul uses this free will prudently and capitalises on the human faculty for metaphysical enquiry, then it can move onwards in its spiritual evolution towards eternity. However, the soul may misuse its free will and desire those bodily indulgences that can be better enjoyed in a sub-human body than in a human body. In such cases, nature facilitates that soul's desire by providing it the corresponding sub-human body. For example, if a human being desires to eat meat inordinately, then nature may provide that soul a lion's body to facilitate that meat-eating desire.

The very presence of free will in humans requires the presence of bodily facilities for executing that free will. This in turn necessitates that the soul be able to go down to sub-human species if it so desires. That's why from the human form the soul's subsequent journey is not automatically upward. It may be downward, wayward, or upward depending on the kind of desires it cultivates.

SOME COMMON OBJECTIONS TO REINCARNATION

Why can't we remember our past lives?

Firstly, it's our tendency to forget; can we remember what we were doing at this very moment one year ago, one month ago or even one week ago? Unlikely. Similarly, our remembering our past lives is highly unlikely. Just because we can't remember a past event doesn't prove the non-occurrence of that event.

Secondly, it's our innate psychological defence mechanism to forget painful incidents; in this very life we get over traumas only by forgetting them with the passage of time. Between our present and past lives lies the trauma of death. Suppose we had died in a car accident and could remember it, we would likely be paranoid of cars throughout our lives. To save us from such psychological malfunctioning, nature arranges to erase our past-life memories.

Thirdly, in our current times, most people are prejudiced against reincarnation by pseudo-scientific materialism and misconceived Semitic dogmas. This leads to the phenomenon that researchers call *childhood suppression of past-life memories*. When children spontaneously recall their past life but find their parents neglectful or sceptical or dismissive of their memories, then such negative reactions discourage them from speaking those memories.

Considering all these filters to past-life memories, what should serve as persuasive evidence is not the forgetfulness of past lives that characterises most people, but the remembrance of past lives that characterises even a few people. And open-minded researchers like Ian Stevenson have documented not just a few but many such cases of spontaneous past-life memories among children who have neither the tendency nor the ability to orchestrate meticulous frauds.

Why are these children able to remember their past lives while most of us can't? It's due to some peculiar karma from their past lives. Our past karma leads to varying memory power even with respect to events and facts of this life: some people have meagre memory power; some, mediocre, and some, photographic. Similarly, some people have no memory of past lives; some, mysterious feelings of déjà vu; and some, clear memories of past lives. Through the past-life memories of these exceptional individuals, God is giving us telltale evidence of reincarnation. As is often said, even one sign is enough for a wise person; now the onus to be wise is upon us.

As we don't remember our past lives, how do we learn anything from them?

The cumulative learning over multiple lives is the assimilation of essential life-lessons about how to act and how to live, not the recollection of specific life-experiences about what we did and when. This focus on principles applies to all cumulative learning, as seen in the following examples of this-life learning:

- Handling boiling water: All of us are cautious when handling boiling water. Do we remember the specific time, place, and circumstance when we learn this caution, possibly the first time when we put our hand in boiling water and burnt it? Unlikely, but that learning did happen due to some experience in a remote forgotten past. Though we have forgotten the details of that experience, we have assimilated its essential lesson: caution in handling boiling water.

- Reading: Every time we read, we utilise hundreds of grammatical rules and thousands of word meanings that we have learnt over many years. Most of us have forgotten the details of when and how we learnt those rules and meanings, but our assimilation of the

183

essence of those learning-experiences is evident in our present ability to read. This focus on principles during cumulative learning is a blessing of nature that ensures our smooth and swift daily functioning. Just imagine how our brain would be cluttered and overloaded if, whenever we started reading, we were swamped by the innumerable specific memories related to each rule and meaning that we were using while reading!

This same mechanism of cumulative learning—assimilation of principles, obliviousness to details—applies to the life-lessons that we have learnt from our past lives. Nature spares us the neural overload that would paralyse us if, whenever we had to do a thing, we had to process all the innumerable specifics of its related past-life experiences.

The *Bhagavad-gita* (15.8) indicates that just as the wind carries from one flower to the next something subtle—a fragrance—the soul carries from one life to another something subtle: the conceptions of life. These conceptions of life are the innate tendencies and natural inclinations that we were born with and that shape our habits of thought, perception and behaviour. Thus, the cumulative learning of our past lives has made us the persons that we see in the mirror.

To summarise, just as the training in this life over many years leads to the subconscious learning of habits and abilities, the training over multiple lifetimes through numerous experiences leads to the subconscious learning of inclinations and tendencies.

Doesn't the growth of population disprove reincarnation? As all souls are eternal and so no new souls

are ever created, doesn't the increase in population imply that new human bodies will eventually run out of souls with which to be incarnated?

Answer: No. This argument is based on two unstated assumptions:

1. Only human beings have souls.
2. All souls exist only in our earthly realm.

But these assumptions are not mandatory. Vedic wisdom delineates an inclusive worldview that refuses to grant monopoly on the soul to either humans alone or to the earth alone. Souls exist in nonhuman bodies and in non-earthly realms of existence.

The *Bhagavad-gita* (2.23) states that the soul is not destroyable by anything material, implying therefore that it can exist in arenas that couldn't sustain life as we know it. The *Gita*'s next verse (02.24) confirms this implication when it states that souls pervade everything; that is, they exist in all parts of the universe. In different parts of the universe, the soul is provided by nature a bodily dress appropriate for its habitat.

The Vedic universe is abuzz with continuous soul traffic: some souls degrade to subhuman species and subterranean regions, some stagnate in human species and on the earthly realm, some rise to supra-human species and celestial regions, and some—a rare few—break entirely free to return to the spiritual world, never to return again. The fuel for this soul traffic is karma: bad karma degrades the soul, mediocre karma stagnates, good karma elevates, and outstanding karma liberates.

As many people today are engaged in mediocre karma, they are likely to be returning—reincarnating—on the human level. Souls from the subhuman bodies and existences naturally rise with due passage of time to human bodies, possibly causing the current population explosion. Even if we take into account that some souls may also be going down to lower species and realms, that still doesn't stop other souls—in greater numbers—to be coming to our realm from other realms. This population increase could be a part of a cosmic plan to give us our karmic dues.

Today, people delight in bad karma, raping nature and abusing her resources for their own selfish greed. The consequent karmic reactions lead to nature withdrawing her gifts, causing the resource crunch plaguing the world today. Another aspect of these karmic reactions could be the current population explosion: increased population and decreased natural resources, when coupled together, deliver karmic dues in an acute way, which is perhaps a jolting yet necessary reminder for humanity to mend its errant ways. Suffice it to say that once its hidden assumptions are pointed out, the population growth argument loses weight. And when we consider the Vedic reincarnation paradigm, it can account persuasively for population growth.

The reincarnation theory claims that we get our characteristics from our own past-life karma, whereas genetics asserts that we inherit our characteristics from our parents, which is what we actually observe in the many physical resemblances among parents and offspring. Don't these observations disprove the reincarnation theory?

No, they don't. The reincarnation theory doesn't claim to contradict or substitute genetics; it supplements genetics and explains many observations that genetics struggles to answer. Genetics holds that we inherit our characteristics from our parents. While the observation of parent-offspring physical resemblances may confirm genetics, many other observations question the completeness of genetic explanations. Here are a few of them:

1. Why do children born in the same family have moral and mental characteristics that differ from each other, from their parents, and even grandparents? For example, why does a child turn out to be an introvert although all other family members are extroverts?

2. Why do twins who are born and bred in similar conditions often have significantly dissimilar behavioural and personality traits? Their genetic inheritance is near identical, yet their natures are sometimes widely different. For example, one twin becomes a starry-eyed artist who doesn't care much for money, whereas the other twin becomes a shrewd businessperson who doesn't care much for art. Why the difference?

   In fact, in the cases of monozygotic twins (twins born from the same embryo, which bifurcates in the early stages of pregnancy), the genes are identical, not just near identical. And yet even such genetically identical twins exhibit dissimilar personality and behavioural traits. Why?

3. Why don't the children of geniuses become geniuses themselves? Often musical maestros can't make their children into outstanding musicians just by begetting them or even by extensively training them. Why?

4. How do children of mediocre parents become geniuses? Many genius artists were born in families that had no above-average artistic talent for several preceding generations, yet they had an inborn talent. Where did their talent come from?

What explanation can genetics provide for the above observations—except for pushing them under the carpet by calling them "anomalies"? But the genetic carpet has too many concealed lumps to be overlooked; these observations demand an additional explanation. That additional explanation is provided by reincarnation.

The *Bhagavad-gita* (15.8) explains that the souls who transmigrate from one body to the next carry with them their conceptions of life, which can be correlated with the mental and moral characteristics. When children are born from parents, their physical bodies come from their parents—and so they resemble their parents' physically, whereas their mental and moral characteristics come from their own past lives—and so these characteristics differ from their parents'.

Applying the *Gita* understanding to geniuses, those souls who have in earlier lives cultivated the self-conceptions of being artists carry to their next bodies that conception along with its associated talents—and so appear precociously talented. Thus, the reincarnation theory doesn't contradict genetics, but supplements it by explaining much that genetics can't explain.

THE ZENITH OF SPIRITUAL EVOLUTION

The human body offers the soul a precious opportunity: the opportunity to reclaim its eternal existence. Regaining eternal life is, according to the Vedic wisdom-tradition, the ultimate purpose of existence. The longing for eternal life is discernible in all species through the ingenious and indefatigable efforts they make to live for as long as possible. However, because everything material is by its very nature temporary, no species can live forever at the material level. Only the human form with its capacity for metaphysical enquiry offers the soul the opportunity to redirect its consciousness from the material level where life is inescapably ephemeral to the spiritual level where life is intrinsically eternal. We humans alone can love the eternal and thereby achieve the eternal.

There, we delight everlastingly in a life of love with the all-attractive, all-loving Absolute Truth. That Absolute Truth is known in the esoteric sections of the Vedic tradition by the inclusive name Krishna, which means "the one who attracts everyone." Krishna is the same Absolute Truth who is known by various names such as Allah, Jehovah, and Buddha in different spiritual traditions. The tradition also offers us the process of *bhakti-yoga* by which we can easily and effectively redirect our desires from matter to the Supreme. Bhakti or love for the divine is the essential process that underlies and unifies the world's great spiritual traditions.

When we are doubly empowered by the knowledge of the goal and the knowledge of the process, we can march confidently on an inner journey that progressively illuminates our heart. When we attain the destination of this journey, the mystery of reincarnation is unravelled; death, transcended; and eternity, reclaimed.

That is life's supreme success.

CHAPTER NINE

THE FREEDOMS OF THE REINCARNATION WORLDVIEW

"Every transformation of man has rested on a new
metaphysical and ideological base . . . a new picture
of the cosmos and the nature of man."
—Historian Lewis Mumford, Transformation of Man

The Vedic literatures of ancient India offer a dramatically different way of looking at the world. Central to the Vedic worldview is an understanding of the soul and its reincarnation. The reincarnation worldview brings about a dramatic and majestic expansion of our conception of life. This expanded understanding of life yields us many freedoms that we normally never access due to a constricted notion of life. This self-improvement and world-improvement potential of the reincarnation-worldview is often missed out by both believers and nonbelievers.

Many believers accept reincarnation as a part of the cultural beliefs that they were born and brought up with, but they often don't recognise the strengths of the reincarnation worldview as compared to the materialist worldview, which consequently remains their operational worldview. Many nonbelievers dismiss belief in reincarnation as new age without considering how it offers insights for solving several challenges that confront all ages and also some challenges that especially bedevil our age.

Let's see how reincarnation helps resolve a fundamental problem that has perplexed humanity throughout history: the problem of the world's inequities.

WHY DIFFERENT STARTING CONDITIONS?

Some of us are born good-looking; some, mediocre-looking. Some of us are born with a phenomenal memory; some, with a below-average memory. These starting conditions often significantly shape the difficulties we face in achieving our life's goals. If I have a below-average memory, and my academic success is measured by exams that test memory, the decks are stacked against me right from the start. If we compare life to a cricket match, then all of us get widely different starting conditions to play the match of life. Many may feel that the match is fixed against them even before it starts.

Why do different people get different starting conditions? The question has no easy answers. Despite the near-impossibility of ascertaining the specific cause of every single suffering that comes upon us, thoughtful people across history and geography have looked for general principles of causality that logically explain life's inequities.

Let us use logic to analyse which worldview best explains these disparities. Which are the worldviews that could be logical candidates for evaluation? If we were to ask why a team got a particular starting score, the various possible explanations would eventually boil down to three: it was determined by chance, or by the organiser, or by the team itself. The same three possibilities emerge when we seek an explanation of life's inequities.

Let's analyse the corresponding worldviews one by one to see which offers the best explanation.

Chance?

This is the materialistic, atheistic worldview which holds that what we are is the result of the chance interactions of natural forces, that one shot at living is all that we ever get, and that we are successes if we mine the maximum material enjoyment out of our brief life-spans.

With such a worldview, the setting for pursuing life's material goals like wealth seems blatantly unfair. Some people are born in heartbreakingly poor families; some, in middle class families with a constant anxiety about paying the bills; some in fabulously wealthy families with plenty of everything material.

Using the cricket analogy, this worldview makes life seem like a one-day cricket tournament in which one team starts with an initial score of 0 runs; another, with a score of 100 runs; and still another, with a score of 200 runs. Why this difference? This worldview answers by saying that there is no answer; some people are lucky, some, unlucky. Period.

Of course, we can console ourselves with the reassurance that, irrespective of where we are now, we can improve our lot. And we can also try to rectify the inequities socio-politically by enacting policies for redistribution of wealth or preferential employment to the economically disadvantaged.

While such reassurances and policies can help to create

a brighter future, they don't at all *rationally explain* the bleak present. The chance-based worldview makes the unlucky feel wronged and helpless. Even the lucky ones end up feeling insecure because their luck may run out at any moment.

Such a worldview is unappealing as it violates our intuitive sense of justice. It is also disempowering as it breeds feelings of helpless victimisation at the hands of blind chance. Most of the people who accept it do so because they don't know of any better alternative. The theistic alternative that they commonly know doesn't seem much better.

Divine Caprice?

This is the worldview of many religions. By adding God to the previous worldview, this worldview posits that the problems of life are moral tests arranged by God to impel us to grow spiritually. While this worldview may explain why life has problems, it doesn't explain why some people have more problems than others. Even if spiritual advancement—and not material aggrandizement—is added to this worldview as the ultimate goal of life, the question of discrimination still remains: why are some people born in devout families that offer abundant opportunities for spiritual growth, and some people born in atheistic families that offer very few, if any, such opportunities?

If God is like the teacher who sets the questions for the test, then this worldview makes God into a discriminatory teacher who arbitrarily gives easy questions to some students and difficult questions to others.

Continuing with the cricket analogy, this worldview makes God the assigner of different starting scores to different teams.

Why does God discriminate like this? This worldview usually answers with some variation of the platitude that God's justice is different from ours. But for those who have been wronged by life, such a rationalisation seems more a covert ploy to get God off the hook than a reasonable explanation. And it is difficult to deny the ring of truth in their resounding retort: God's justice may be different from ours, but it should be different in the sense of being better than ours, not worse.

It is a sad fact of history that the demand for faith in such a capricious "God" has caused millions of intelligent, sincere people to balk. Thousands have even taken what seemed to them the next logical step and embraced full-scale atheism. Given that they had to make the difficult choice between the two unpalatable options of mundane chance and divine caprice, their decision is understandable.

Understandable, but ill-informed. Because there is a third option.

Multi-life progression

The third option is the Vedic worldview that incorporates reincarnation and karma into a complete Weltanschauung that is empowering, both individually and socially.

The Vedic reincarnation worldview explains that all of us are eternal souls who have reincarnated through many lives in the past and will also reincarnate through as many future lives as are necessary for our spiritual growth. These multiple reincarnations provide us opportunities for self-education that culminates in graduation into eternal life. The qualification for graduation is the development of the supreme virtue of selfless love for God and all his children. Those who don't graduate by the end of their present life get further chances in their future lives, where their starting point is determined by the deeds of their present life. Extending the same principle backwards in time, the individual starting points that we got in this life were determined by where we had left off in our previous life.

The reincarnation-based worldview enables us to see that the diversity among people is like the diversity among students who are in different classes in a university. Just as different students get different exams according to what is required to raise them from their present class to the next, all of us face different problems in life according to what is best suited to raise us from our present moral and spiritual level to the next.

Going back to the cricket analogy, life is like a multi-innings test match where our present lifetime is only one innings. The differing initial scores that different teams start off with are determined not by arbitrary fluke or fiat but by the lead (or the lag) they had themselves acquired in their previous innings. Life's match is ultimately fair because life gives us what we have earned; if the match seems fixed then it is we ourselves who have fixed it.

Of course, there are subtleties and nuances to this worldview, but overall it offers us a coherent explanation for life's disparities. When contrasted with the irrational beliefs that we are prenatal victims of either mundane chance or divine caprice, the Vedic explanation that we are the intermediate products of our own past choices shines with the light of rationality. And the knowledge that the present "I" is an intermediate product—not the final product—that can be refined by present choices is definitely empowering.

REDEFINING OUR RELATIONSHIPS

The reincarnation worldview is also socially empowering, for it transforms our vision of the universe from that of a jungle to that of a university. This educational vision of the universe infuses our relationships with a mood of learning and sharing instead of a mood of fighting and grabbing.

By redefining our view of the world as a university and of all living beings as fellow-students, the reincarnation-based worldview helps us to see those less endowed with qualities and abilities than us with sympathy rather than scorn; they are like kindergarten students who deserve the encouragement, not the scorn, of college students. The awareness that we too were at that level once inspires us to extend a lifting hand rather than a pushing hand.

This worldview also engenders respect for those better endowed than us; they have earned their PhDs by diligent study in the same university where we are striving to pass through junior college. As the same spiritual expressway that they took is open to us, we feel inspired to accelerate our journey along that way by learning from them instead of getting stuck where we are by envying them. We don't need to compete even against those who are our equals; our success does not require their failure, as it often does in material endeavours like sports, where the victory of one team requires the defeat of another or academics, where the limited number of seats in a prestigious university necessitates that students edge out their competitors.

In joyful contrast, spiritual endeavours depend only on our sincerely striving to develop a loving service attitude—irrespective of whether our equals become better than us. In the spiritual world, the original home of the soul, there is no competition for limited seats; all of us have our own individual seat in the spiritual world reserved inalienably for us, just waiting for us to reclaim them by making sufficient spiritual advancement. Thus, our life's cricket match is not against others, but against our own lower self, which drags us down into irrational, growth-stunting choices. And when we start playing the match against our lower self earnestly, we experience how the Vedic worldview is practically empowering.

EXPERIENTIAL CONFIRMATION

The philosophical worldview that intelligibly answers questions, which have otherwise baffled the human intellect, is just the beginning of the gifts on offer for humanity from the Vedic wisdom-tradition. For those spiritually adventurous enough, this worldview becomes the intellectual launching pad for the experiential techniques of yoga. Bhakti-yoga gives experience of inner spiritual fulfilment that, for the sincere yogi, becomes the experiential confirmation of the reincarnation philosophy.

The devotional classic in the Vedic library, the *Bhagavata Purana*, explains this through an analogy that all of us can relate to: "Devotion, direct experience of God, and detachment from other things—these three occur simultaneously for one who has taken shelter of God, in the same way that pleasure, nourishment, and relief from hunger come simultaneously and increasingly, with each bite, for a person engaged in eating."

The spiritual satisfaction coming from direct experience of the divine and the resulting detachment from worldly things helps us see the inequities of life as relatively unimportant: they are temporary, superficial to our spiritual essence, and inconsequential in our pursuit of everlasting spiritual fulfilment.

Moreover, wherever we may presently be along the spiritual continuum of life, the cultivation of spiritual awareness offers the best pathway to spiritual perfection. It empowers us to break free from self-defeating patterns of thought and behaviour that imprison us in injurious choices. It also blesses us with the inner clarity and purity by which we can receive divine guidance and make the best choices. Pertinently the *Bhagavad-gita* (10.10) assures, "To those who are constantly devoted to serving me [God] with love, I give the understanding by which they can come to me."

Overall, the reincarnation-based worldview empowers us to make the best sense out of the seeming senselessness of life. Not only that, the insight that life's disparities are neither arbitrary nor discriminatory, but are progressive and tailor-made, transforms life into an exciting and fulfilling adventure. When we try to fix the match of our life ourselves as most of us have been trying until now, we end up making a mess out of it—sooner or later. But when we bring Krishna and his wisdom into our life, he guides us to fix it—for good.

Beyond explaining the problem of evil, the reincarnation worldview offers several other invaluable freedoms:

1. **Freedom from Unidimensional Materialism**
   The notion that there's nothing more to our self than the material body shrinks our options for happiness to just one stereotyped track: materialism. Let's look at the emotional, economic, and ecological consequences of this shrinkage of our options for happiness.

Emotional consequences

When we believe that our only gateways to happiness are those offered by the material body, the full force of our craving for happiness gets centred on pandering to bodily impulses. But all material pleasures are inescapably limited by our body's finite capacity for pleasure. Consequently, our material indulgences, no matter how extravagant, leave us feeling dissatisfied and tormented by the desire for more.

Additionally, because we neglect our spiritual side, we feel a gnawing sense of emptiness and meaninglessness eating us from within. Contemporary Vedic savants refer to this unfortunate emotional and spiritual malnourishment metaphorically, using a bird-cage metaphor that can be called "polishing the cage, famishing the bird." The body is like a cage and the soul, the bird within. Those who cater to the body's needs but neglect the soul's needs are, metaphorically speaking, polishing the cage while letting the bird within starve.

Economic consequences

This bird-cage metaphor for the lopsidedness of our quest for happiness may seem quaintly poetic, but the real-life ramifications of this lopsidedness are far from trivial. At the material level, human efforts for happiness are repeatedly hamstrung by a perpetual economic perplexity. This perplexity centres on the attempt to satisfy the unlimited desires of human beings with the limited resources of the world.

Unidimensional materialism aggravates this problem because it equates happiness with possession and consumption of these limited resources. As both the haves and the have-nots want to be happy, this materialist definition of happiness accentuates the stark contrast and the simmering conflict between the haves and the have-nots. Driven by such a material definition of happiness the haves crave for more, no matter how much they have. And the have-nots too labour on the same dead-end materialist track trodden by the haves.

Ecological consequences

Unidimensional materialism causes people's material desires to skyrocket, thereby placing an unsustainable pressure on the finite resources of the world. This pressure has contributed significantly to, if not caused primarily, the massive ecological problems threatening humanity today, be they pollution of land, water, and air depletion of non-renewable fossil fuels, renewable forest cover, or the spectre of climate change. Thus, unidimensional materialism, by its emotional, economic, and ecological consequences misdirects, frustrates, and perverts our quest for happiness.

The reincarnation worldview protects us from such a tragic lopsidedness in our quest for happiness. These insights help us harmonise our priority with reality: just as the bird is more important than the cage, the soul is more important than the body. We see the pragmatic value of giving spiritual development its due in terms of our time, thought, and energy. Refusing to let materialism unwarrantedly monopolise our search for happiness, we strike a prudent and productive balance between our material and spiritual sides, and benefit from the emotional, economic, and ecological spinoffs of that holistic balance.

2. **Freedom from Body-Based Discrimination**

Humanity today is torn due to conflicts originating in differences over nationality, race, class, caste, religion, colour, and so forth. Many of us may intuitively feel that these differences can be resolved or at least minimised, if the conflicting sides could see their mutual similarities. Unfortunately, this feeling has a high casualty rate in the journey from theory to practice; our attempts to see similarities with others get frequently subverted by the glaring and undeniable differences that do exist between us at the bodily level. The reincarnation worldview empowers the attempt to see similarities. How? By raising our vision from the level of sentimentality to the level of reality. The sentiment that all of us are similar is noble and desirable but it is difficult to sustain when confronted with the hard-nosed reality of dissimilarities that do separate us at the bodily level.

The reincarnation worldview helps us understand that underlying these undeniable dissimilarities is a unifying reality: all of us are souls, and all souls are essentially similar in nature. Once we grasp the reality that our body is peripheral to our core identity, all bodily differences stand exposed as insubstantial and inconsequential. We may have been born and bred in different races, classes, nations, cultures, or even religions, but all these varying labels apply only to our bodily shells. Beyond these differing shells are our similar souls. Thus, the reincarnation worldview has the potential to free everyone everywhere from the divisiveness inherent in the bodily conception of life and to unify all of humanity on the non-sectarian foundation of spiritual reality.

In fact, the inclusiveness of the Vedic worldview embraces in its fold not only all human beings but also all nonhuman living beings.

The *Bhagavad-gita* (5.18) shares this all-embracing vision of those individuals who have realised the soul: "The humble sages, by virtue of true knowledge, see with equal vision a learned and gentle intellectual, a cow, an elephant, a dog, and an uncultured person."

As discussed in the previous chapter, the Vedic wisdom-tradition doesn't entertain the sectarian human arrogance of claiming monopoly on the soul; it explains that the souls that animate human and nonhuman bodies are essentially similar. This Vedic understanding helps us see in a fresh and meaningful light the findings of ethologists that animals live, love, play, and cry just like us humans. It also offers a philosophical foundation for the animal rights movement that opposes humanity's self-serving vision of the animal world as meant for human exploitation and consumption.

In fact, the reincarnation worldview makes obvious the short-sightedness and counter-productiveness of body-based animosity. A person who lays waste to the environment for materialist gains may well be reborn in that ravaged environment and be compelled to endure the misery of scarcity and pollution. A person who targets an enemy due to feelings of mass hatred may well end up being reborn in the enemy camp and becoming the target of the same hatred. A person who feasts on slaughtered animal flesh may well become in a future life the target of the slaughterer's blade.

In addition to removing negative prejudices, the reincarnation worldview can positively impact our personal relationships, for it transforms our vision of the universe from a jungle to a university. We no longer see life as a horizontal competition in the material realm for its finite pleasures; instead, we see life as a vertical progression towards the spiritual realm for its infinite rewards. We understand that our progress on the vertical axis depends on our assimilation of the lessons of spiritual wisdom and divine love. When we realise that all of us are fellow-students in learning these lessons, this vision inspires us to relate with others in a learning and sharing mood, not a fighting and grabbing mood.

Thus, the reincarnation worldview offers us profound power—individually, socially, and globally— to free ourselves from the body-based prejudices that threaten to tear our contemporary world apart.

3. Freedom from the Fear of Death

The prospect of death is so frightening for most of us that conscious contemplation on it threatens to fill us with despair. That's why we often prefer to live in denial of death—if not consciously then at least subconsciously. But the reincarnation worldview opens for us an alternative beyond despair and denial.

To see how, let's analyse the fear of death in terms of the three phases of time—past, present, and future—centred on the event of death:

i. **Past**

One reason we find death frightening is that it involves losing all the things for which we have given our past; it threatens to separate us from everything that we have struggled to accumulate and everyone that we have strived to love.

The reincarnation worldview encourages us to intelligently distribute our life's energy between our material obligations and our spiritual necessities. The energy that we invest in attending to our spiritual needs leads to the evolution of our consciousness. As consciousness is an integral, inalienable characteristic of the soul, the refined consciousness that we have developed goes with us in our post-mortem journey unlike our material assets that stay behind.

The *Bhagavad-gita* (2.40) confirms that the inner assets we accumulate along the spiritual journey are never lost or even decreased. And ultimately it is the state of our consciousness—our state of mind and state of being—that determines our happiness. Thus, moulding our life according to the reincarnation worldview ensures that we don't go empty-handed at the time of death, but carry with us the inner asset that matters most for our happiness. And the assurance that we will be able to carry our most precious asset with us after death greatly decreases its fear.

ii. **Present**

Another reason why we find death fearsome is because it forces us to witness and endure the breakdown of our physical body, an experience that we dread and view as excruciating. When we misidentify ourselves with our body, then its destruction seems to us to be the destruction of our very selves.

This perception compounds our fear because it makes death seem emotionally horrifying in addition to being physically excruciating. But when we understand our identity as indestructible souls who are untouched by the destruction of the body, then we become free from much of the horror associated with death.

The breakdown of the body is obviously not pleasant for anyone, but when we are spiritually aware we no longer see bodily breakdown as the self-exterminating disaster that it had seemed earlier. Knowing that the body is a vehicle for the soul, we see its breakdown as a discomfort, just as we would see the breakdown of our car as a discomfort. This educated downsizing of bodily destruction from a disaster to a discomfort further decreases the fear associated with death.

iii. **Future**

A third reason we fear death is because we just don't know what will happen to us after death: whether we will be annihilated or, if we survive, where we will go— whether we will be taken to a better place or a worse place, or stay in suspended animation in no man's land.

The reincarnation worldview helps us see death as not a termination but a transition: a transition to continued existence in another sphere. In the book of life, we see death not as a period but as a comma.

The awareness that life is an unending continuum in which death is a milestone that we have passed many times in the past helps expand the horizons of our consciousness far beyond death in this lifetime to the ultimate destination of eternal happiness.

Moreover, the reincarnation worldview helps us prepare not only for the transition but also for the destination. If we refine our consciousness by spiritual practice during our life, then we ensure an improved station for ourselves in our next life. And if we harmonise our consciousness fully with our innate spiritual nature, then we can even look forward to attaining an eternal post-mortem destination.

Thus, the knowledge that our spiritual core is inviolable by death enables us to face death with courage and dignity. But the dividends from the reincarnation worldview go far beyond facing death with courage to preparing for it with confidence. When we understand the principles that determine our post-mortem destination, we can confidently prepare for attaining a desirable destination by harmonising our consciousness and lifestyle with those principles.

The *Bhagavad-gita* (8.4-5) outlines these principles: our state of mind at the moment of death determines our state of being after death. So, if we remember

Krishna at the moment of death, we attain his eternal abode after death, which is life's ultimate attainment.

4. **Freedom from the Agony of Bereavement**

One of life's greatest agonies apart from our own death is the demise of a loved one. Our sense of bereavement is in itself anguishing, but it is exacerbated by the feeling of helplessness at not being able to do anything for our loved one, to not know whether they even exist. In such heart-wrenching times, the reincarnation worldview can provide immense solace. The knowledge that our loved one continues to exist at some other place brings relief from the torment of ignorance. The further knowledge that spiritual connections continue beyond the constraints of time and space, and so our prayers and meditation for the wellbeing of others can help them wherever they are is positively empowering. And if we are fortunate enough to be guided by the reincarnation worldview before the bereavement, then we know how to assist our loved one in making that fateful transition gracefully and auspiciously. When we share spiritual wisdom and devotional solace with them, the intense spiritual bonding that develops during the final days often becomes one of life's most enriching experiences.

To conclude, the reincarnation worldview offers us a reasonable explanation for the world's inequities and freedom from unidimensional materialism, body-based discrimination, fear of death, and the agony of bereavement. Ours is an age characterised by the zeal for freedom and the willingness to sacrifice anything for the sake of freedom. Maybe it's time to exercise that zeal for gaining all these freedoms and sacrificing whatever preconceptions come in the way.

It is fitting to sign off with an insightful comment of Austrian philosopher Rudolf Steiner: "Just as an age was once ready to receive the Copernican theory of the universe, so is our age ready for the idea of reincarnation to be brought into the general consciousness of humanity."

THE COMEBACK OF THE SOUL

"If a non-material soul is the source of consciousness in the material body, how do the two radically different entities—one non-material and the other material—interact?"

This question has found few, if any, satisfactory answers in Western intellectual history for the last several centuries. The absence of plausible answers has, over time, led to the exile of the soul from mainstream intellectual discourse.

In this section we will discuss how the soul is making a comeback due to several significant scientific developments that have reshaped the context of the spirit-matter interaction problem.

THE EXILE

Let's begin by clarifying a few basic terms. Those thinkers who hold that there are two distinct realms of reality—spiritual and material—are called dualists. They are often contrasted with materialists who hold that there is only one level of reality: material.

A prominent dualist thinker in the western intellectual tradition was the seventeenth century French philosopher-mathematician Rene Descartes. He proposed that mind and matter interact through the pineal gland, which was the brain's only symmetrical part without a left and right counterpart. This explanation was rejected by most subsequent thinkers, and the interaction problem remained unsolved.

Meanwhile advances in science led to the explanation of much of material reality in material terms, that is, in terms of the interaction of material particles and forces. Generalizing this finding, many scientists started holding material reality to be causally complete. That is, they held that all effects at the material level could be traced to causes at the material level. This proposed causal completeness left no room for a non-material soul to exert any influence on the material level.

Thus, the soul became, in the scientific worldview, causally impotent and thereby irrelevant. For materialists, downgrading the soul from causal impotence to ontological non-existence required only a small push: "If the soul doesn't matter—if it can't affect matter—then why believe it exists?"

THE QUAKE

At the dawn of the twentieth century, many materialist scientists, being buoyed by the seeming causal completeness of material science, were euphoric that they were closing in on a clear understanding of everything that there was to know. But subsequent developments, especially with the emergence of quantum physics, led to the contravening of many major notions that had been held as incontrovertible by pre-existing

Newtonian physics. The consequences were far-reaching, even earth-shattering.

Cultural historian Richard Tarnas in his book *The Passion of the Western Mind* quotes the reactions of two of the greatest scientists of the twentieth century.

- "All my attempts to adapt the theoretical foundation of physics to this knowledge failed completely. It was as if the ground had been pulled out from under one, with no firm foundation to be seen anywhere upon which one could have built." – Albert Einstein

- "The foundations of physics have started moving . . . [and] this motion has caused the feeling that the ground would be cut from science." – Werner Heisenberg

The details of this quake are technical and complex, but the one significant consequence of quantum physics relevant to our discussion is that consciousness suddenly became acceptable, even essential, in the scientific picture of reality.

According to the standard Copenhagen interpretation of quantum physics, a non-material conscious observer became essential to resolve the probabilities of the wave function into a definite eventuality. The fact that a conscious observer played a critical, possibly indispensable, role in quantum physics undercut the previously cherished materialist assumptions of science. Nobel Laureate physicist Eugene Wigner declared that materialism—at least with regard to consciousness—is not "logically consistent with present quantum mechanics." Similarly, Sir Rudolf Peierls, another eminent twentieth-century physicist, commenting on the implications of quantum mechanics, asserted, "The premise that you can describe in terms of physics the whole function of a human being . . . including [his] knowledge, and [his] consciousness, is untenable."

Of course, the technicalities of what exact role consciousness plays in quantum physics or how exactly it plays that role is far from clear. But what is quite clear is that consciousness is no longer taboo within the scientific sketch of the world—thanks to the developments in physics, consciousness now has a foothold, even a stronghold. Of course the problem of how consciousness interacts with matter still remains.

PROBLEMS EVERYWHERE

But then, this might be a problem not with consciousness but with materialist science. After all, materialist science struggles to explain not just consciousness-matter interaction but also matter-matter interaction.

According to mainstream physics, material bodies comprise electrically charged particles whose mutual interaction is mediated by electromagnetic fields. This mediation, physicist Stephen Barr underscores, in the magazine *First Things*, Jan 2010 issue, is a matter of unacknowledged ignorance for physics: "The charged particles affect the fields and the fields affect the particles. By what "means" or "mechanism" this happens, physics does not say." All that physics says is that the presence of electromagnetic fields affects the charges in ways that are described by certain equations. And the presence of the charges affects the electromagnetic fields in ways that are described by another set of equations.

Put bluntly, physics posits two types of entities—particles and fields—and provides a mathematical description of their interaction. But a mathematical description is no substitute for an ontological explanation.

Thus, despite the increasing complexity of their equations, physicists today are fundamentally at a position similar to Newton's when he postulated his precise equations describing the interaction of mass and gravity. He famously admitted in his *Principia*, "I have not been able to discover the cause of those properties of gravity . . . and I frame no hypotheses . . . to us it is enough that gravitational forces really exist, and act according to [these] laws."

Ignorance of a precise interactional mechanism was not used to bar gravity from the world of science. Why, then, should the ignorance of a precise interactional mechanism be used to bar consciousness?

Additionally, the problem of an elusive interactional mechanism dogs not just dualists but also materialists. Materialist scientists assume that as there is no separate realm of spirit, consciousness must emerge from the electrochemical activity of neuronal cells. They hold that as consciousness is ultimately material, they will be able to explain its interaction with neuronal cells.

Even if we grant, for argument's sake, that consciousness emerges from the brain, the two—our conscious feelings and the corresponding electrochemical brain states—are so utterly dissimilar that the claim that the first emerges from the other is a mere assertion with no inkling of the actual mechanism involved.

Consider for example, the proposition of materialist neuroscience that the subject feels bored or apathetic because of a below-average concentration in the brain of a molecule called dopamine. However, dopamine is nothing but a certain arrangement of eight carbon atoms, eleven hydrogen atoms, one nitrogen atom, and two oxygen atoms. How exactly does its decrease cause boredom? How precisely does carbon, hydrogen, nitrogen, oxygen, or their combination remove boredom? Few if any, neuroscientists ascribe emotional power to these fundamental elements. How then can it be ascribed to their combination or to the decreased presence of that combination?

Probing deeper, what exactly does materialist science know about the relationship between dopamine concentrations and mental states? All that it knows is that there is an observed correlation between the two. That this correlation is a causal connection is an unsubstantiated and unexplained faith-claim of materialism. Poking at the clay feet of such claims American philosopher David Berlinski, in his book *The Devil's Delusion* asks, "How a craving for raspberry Jell-O might be located within the human brain . . . Perhaps it involves neurons devoted to gelatin? I am asking in a spirit of honest inquiry."

THE FORECAST

Will future scientific research make the sun shine brighter for materialist neuroscientists? Unlikely. Philosophy professor Colin McGinn states succinctly what the sunshine is revealing: "The more we know of the brain, the less it looks like a device for creating consciousness: it's just a big collection of biological cells and a blur of electrical activity." (New Statesman, 20 Feb 2012)

No matter how much we increase our knowledge of which brain activity corresponds with which mental states, that increased knowledge will add only to details; it will not even address, leave alone illuminate the principle of how brain activity produces mental states.

In fact, the sunshine of scientific developments is revealing the territory to be opposite to what materialists had expected. Materialists base their attempts at reductive interpretations of consciousness on the thoroughgoing materialism of physics, for physics is generally considered the most fundamental of all the sciences.

But over the last century, the thoroughgoing materialism of physics has been going out of the developmental door to the scientific museums. As discussed earlier, physics is being led away from materialism by the force of its own development. However, materialist neuroscientists seem to be utterly out of step with these developments. They are rigorously trying to apply to consciousness the hardline materialism that physics has found to be inapplicable even to matter.

Paul Davies, in his book *God and The New Physics*, quotes American biophysicist Harold J. Morowitz on this anachronistic trend: "It is as if the two disciplines were on fast-moving trains, going in opposite directions and not noticing what is happening across the tracks." Mario Beauregard, in his book *The Spiritual Brain*, underscores the implications for biology of the changes in physics through a rhetorical question: "If physics fails to support biology, which discipline should rethink its position—physics or biology?"

Thus, the sunshine of scientific developments is darkening the horizons for materialist explanations of consciousness and is brightening the pathway for non-materialist explanations.

A MODEL

For dualism, the sunshine has illuminated not just its conceptual landscape but also its demonstrable landscape. Technological advances have provided a model for consciousness-matter interaction in the form of a virtual reality system. In such a system, the user controls the actions of a virtual object or person through an appropriate interface. Within the virtual world, though actions happen as per the laws of physics, the system is so arranged that the consciousness of the person outside the virtual world determines the actions inside it.

Might such a thing be happening in real-life? Yes is the emphatic assertion of Vedic wisdom. It holds that our material existence is illusory, akin to a virtual reality. We are souls, spiritual beings who belong originally to a non-material realm but are presently functioning at the material level. The *Bhagavad-gita* (13.34) indicates that the channelling of the non-material soul's consciousness to the material body happens through projection, just as the sun's light projects through the universe.

How the soul's consciousness is projected into the material realm is elucidated in the *Bhagavata Purana*, canto four with an intricate allegory. In his book *Human Devolution* Michael Cremo uses this allegory to explain how our present material realm might be seen as a virtual reality. Central to understanding this model is the underlying vision of reality as having three levels:

1. Material or gross material,
2. Mental or subtle material, and
3. Conscious or spiritual.

In this model, the mind is not equated with consciousness, as is done in most Western intellectual discourse. Instead, the mind is seen as a subtle material object that bridges the gap between nonmaterial consciousness and gross matter. In Cremo's words, "the mind might be compared to multimedia computer software capable of integrating audio and visual materials into a single display, making use of a variety of inputs and source materials."

Just as the user of a virtual reality system identifies with a character in the virtual world through a suitable interface, the soul identifies with a gross body in the material realm through the interface of the mind. The designer of the virtual reality system makes the necessary linking arrangements for the clients to use it. Similarly, Vedic wisdom posits that the designer of all of existence, the supreme consciousness, is personally present with every soul as a proximate neighbour overseeing the linking arrangements necessary for the soul to function in the material realm (*Bhagavad-gita* 13.23). Additionally, the supreme consciousness is seen as the source and sustainer of both the material, and spiritual realms, (*Bhagavad-gita* 7.6) and so is entirely capable of straddling the two realms and aiding the soul in doing the same.

Thus, the Vedic model provides two critical concepts for bridging the valley between matter and spirit that has swallowed western dualists since the time of Descartes:

1. A subtle mind as an instrumental link
2. The supreme consciousness as the designer and overseer of both realms

The comparison of material existence with virtual reality is not a newfangled scientific superimposition on Vedic wisdom. Rather, it is just a scientific rendition of one of its central tenets: Maya. This word is sometimes loosely translated as illusion, but it actually connotes the entire complex system that brings about the illusory misidentification of consciousness with matter. Thus, the concept of Maya intrinsically parallels the concept of virtual reality.

Richard L Thompson, a Cornell-educated mathematician, has devoted a full book *Maya: The World as a Virtual Reality* for exploring the concept of Maya scientifically. He outlines how the metaphor of a virtual reality can help integrate a broad spectrum of ideas from mainstream science, paranormal science, and philosophy into a coherent vision of reality.

Some may dismiss or downplay such models for consciousness-matter interaction because they are not yet mainstream science. These naysayers might do well to remember that frequently science's greatest breakthroughs came about because it focused on the fringes.

At the start of the twentieth century, the edifice of classical physics seemed strong and imposing, situated on the bedrock of Newtonian mechanics. But on the fringes remained the problem associated with explaining blackbody radiation. It was only because Nobel Laureates such as Neils Bohr and a galaxy of open-minded scientists focused on that problem that the whole new field of quantum physics developed. A similar openness to the problem of consciousness-matter interaction may open new vistas in science's further progress.

A PERSONAL QUANTUM LEAP

Vedic wisdom focuses primarily on providing spiritual principles and practices meant to guide the soul out of the virtual reality and back to the actual reality, where existence is spiritual and eternal. In addition to its spiritual essence, Vedic wisdom also offers a sophisticated analysis of the material level and the modality of the entanglement of soul with matter. This analysis holds the dual potential of explanation and expansion: it provides insights that explain many perplexities that presently baffle materialist science, and it expands the frontiers of science beyond the confines of materialism.

Such is the conclusion of American physicist Henry Stapp who wrote a monograph on Vedic ontology as presented in one of its most prominent traditions known as *Gaudiya Vaishnavism*. In his monograph entitled *A report on the Gaudiya Vaishnava Vedanta form of Vedic ontology*, Stapp concludes by stating, "It is worth that although the ideas outlined above were inspired by the theistic GVV [*Gaudiya Vaishnava Vedanta*], they involve in principle, contrary to what might be expected from a theistic framework, an *extension* or *enlargement* of the mathematical features of the theory beyond those encompassed by contemporary physics."

For those interested in analysing technically vexing intellectual problems like spirit-matter interaction, Vedic wisdom offers a rich intellectual resource. Additionally, for those interested in practical application, it offers even richer transformational resources for restoring in our own lives a healthy material-spiritual balance. And we can use these practical processes even if their theoretical underpinnings aren't still fully comprehended by science.

The principle of practically utilizing concepts whose working mechanisms are yet not clearly understood has respectable precedents in science, especially in the medical field. University of Virginia Psychiatrist Jim Tucker points out that such utilisation has been to our benefit, not our detriment: "We are fortunate that the field of medicine has not waited for mechanisms to be uncovered before taking advantage of effective treatments, since physicians have successfully used numerous medications before knowing their mechanisms of action."

If we adopt the same pragmatism for Vedic insights about the soul, we will experience quantum leaps in our personal spiritual growth.

ꕯꕥꕯ

ON MACHINE CONSCIOUSNESS

Computers seem to be getting faster and better all the time. As they incorporate more and more diverse functionalities, some people feel that they will also integrate functionality for consciousness. In this section, we will investigate this possibility by analysing what computers essentially do, what their capabilities include and exclude, and what this implies for consciousness research.

THE ESSENTIALS

The conceptual pathway for modern computing was paved by the British logician Alan Turing in 1936 when he published his first papers on computability. He proposed an imaginary machine that could smoothly and suavely imitate the logical functions of the human mind. This machine, known since as the Turing machine, outlines the basic principles that underlie the functioning of computers of all levels of sophistication.

By understanding the structuring and functioning of a Turing machine, we can understand what computers essentially do.

The basic components of a Turing machine are:

1. A tape divided into squares
2. A reading head capable of going through a finite number of distinct physical states
3. A finite number of symbols, usually 0's and 1's.

Actions of a Turing machine:

1. Recognise symbols on the tape, one square at a time
2. Write or erase symbols from the square it is scanning
3. Change its internal state
4. Move to the left or right of the square it is scanning, one at a time.

This is all that a Turing machine can do. In fact, it cannot do any of these things; being a mere mechanism, it is by default passive. Only when activated and directed by a program can it do any of the above actions.

BEYOND FACE VALUES

No computer can do anything essentially different from what a Turing machine does. What computers can do is perform these basic operations at phenomenal speeds, thereby processing information much faster than us humans. Their super-human information processing capacities often makes many of us see them with awe. Consequently, we don't see them as tools for our heads, just as hammers are tools for our hands. Instead, we see computers as our peers and maybe even as our superiors. Naturally, when we are told by some technologists that future computers will embody consciousness, some of us take their words at face value.

Face values can be deceptive in any field—and all the more so in the field of computer science. Why? Because the awe-inspiring face of computers can easily cause us to overvalue them. To help us go beyond the face to the value, we need an embodiment of the Turing machine that is less awe-inspiring. One such awe-uninspiring embodiment is the abacus. This primitive device uses counters that slide on rods or in grooves to perform basic arithmetic functions.

It is critical to bear in mind that both a tacky abacus and a trendy computer, being embodiments of the same Turing machine, run on the same essential principles. Both perform the same fundamental actions. So the prospect of a future computer becoming conscious is, in principle, no different from the prospect of a future abacus becoming conscious. But the prospect of a conscious abacus strikes us as not just distinctly implausible, but as downright imbecile.

Recognizing the unapparent similarities between an abacus and a computer de-glamorises our vision of computers: we understand all that computers do is high-speed symbol shuffling. The idea that increasing the speed of the shuffling may produce consciousness is as untenable as the idea that increasing the speed of motion of the counters on an abacus may produce consciousness. Only when the faces are unmasked do the values become obvious.

BRUTE FORCE: THE KEY TO ILLUSION

Lest doubts that computers might be up to something more still linger in our minds, let's consider an extract from an article in the *American Scientist* by science writer Brian Hayes: "We have many clever gadgets, but it's not at all clear they add up to a 'thinking machine.' Their methods and inner mechanisms seem nothing like human mental processes. Perhaps we should not be bragging about how smart our machines have become; rather, we should marvel at how much those machines accomplish without any genuine intelligence." (American Scientist Vol. 100, July-August 2012)

"Without any genuine intelligence" can act as the decisive doubt-killer. Hayes explains that the success of computers in everything from data search to chess playing has come from a brute-force approach. This approach uses computers with vast memory and superfast processing speeds to check whichever string of symbols best match the specified string of symbols without even attempting to comprehend either of the strings.

Due to the development of faster processors and high-storage memory chips, the speed of this brute-force approach has equalled and even exceeded the speed of human logical processing. But such computer processing leaves out entirely the whole gamut of conscious experiences that accompany our logical processing. Let's look at just two features of those conscious experiences: meanings and feelings.

Where's the Meaning?

To understand the essential principles, let's again start with a simple avatar of the Turing machine. Suppose we press "3" on a calculator twice with a "+" sign in between. The calculator displays "6." As far as the calculator is concerned, it has simply received pushes on its keypads, shuttled symbols in its chips, and turned on tiny lights on its display panel.

What makes the lit shapes on its display panel meaningful is the presence of a conscious person who interprets those shapes as an answer to a question that he or she had posed.

What does the calculator understand? Neither the question nor the answer. Neither the concept of numbers nor the concept of addition. Neither the meaning of the keys pressed nor the significance of the patterns displayed. In short, nothing. Being a mere physical device the calculator is incapable of any understanding whatsoever.

As computers run on the same principles as calculators, they too are incapable of any understanding, no matter how speedy and sophisticated they become at symbol shuffling.

Attempts to integrate understanding into computer information processing programs such as language translation have been so unsuccessful that they have been abandoned in favour of brute force approaches.

Who's Feeling?

Sports evoke intense emotions: the winners are elated; the losers, devastated. Computers have learnt and even mastered several sports like checkers and chess.

In 1996, the chess-playing computer Deep Blue gave the blues to the then world chess champion Gary Kasparov. Since that landmark in computing, sports-playing computers have only become faster and better.

In 2011, Watson, a computer designed to play a TV quiz competition called *Jeopardy!* created a global sensation by defeating the 74-time *Jeopardy!* champion Ken Jennings who has won a total of $3,172,700 on the show and holds the all-time records for total game show earnings. After the match Jennings said that he felt "insignificant", and computer-scientist David Ferrucci, the leader of the team that had made Watson reported being delighted.

But Watson, which had actually "won" the competition, was not delighted; in fact, it had no emotions at all. It had simply done text processing in accordance with its sophisticated program that mechanically retrieves relevant documents, extracts the named-entities in the documents and prioritises the named-entities according to the question. Watson, by functioning according to its program, had "played" *Jeopardy!* and "won" the competition without experiencing any of the essential emotions that a human player goes through: excitement, disappointment, anticipation, exhilaration, and so on.

Watson's victory demonstrates that, even when computers have abilities that surpass human abilities, they still can't experience any emotions at all. If sci-fi movie images of laughing Frankenstein monsters and crying Terminators haunt us, we can exorcise them by contemplating that they are essentially Turing machines. If such contemplation doesn't help we can remember that sci-fi creatures are essentially no different from abacuses.

A NEW FUNDAMENTAL REALITY

The analysis of these two features of consciousness—meanings and feelings—reveals a common pattern. Both features are absent in the machines but can be traced back to conscious humans, who are either the makers or the users of those machines.

When it comes to meanings and feelings, all of us know that we have them. For researchers knocking at the door of consciousness in human beings, the lights are clearly on—someone is surely at home. But who is it that is at home? And where? Where in conscious humans is the locus of consciousness?

MIGHT IT BE THE BRAIN?

Cognitive scientists often consider the computer to be a model of the human brain. By parity of reasoning, if consciousness is not to be found in the computer, then it is not to be found in the brain either. After all, both are essentially material tools for information processing: the computer uses digital circuitry and the brain uses neural circuitry. Just as the computer needs a conscious observer to make sense of the data it processes and displays, so would the brain.

Of course, we might argue that such an observing entity would also need another conscious observer, thereby leading to an infinite regress.

However, this infinite regress results only due to a prior commitment to the ideology of materialism. If no such ideological commitments bias our perspectives, we can readily see the way out of the regress: recognise consciousness as a fundamental materially-irreducible reality in the universe. To grasp the rationale for this way out of the regress let's consider two questions: Is consciousness real? And is it reducible?

The reality of consciousness is undeniable because the very act of denying its existence proves its existence. How? Denial is a conscious act; we need consciousness to deny that we have consciousness. A table cannot deny that it has consciousness because it doesn't have the consciousness that is essential for making the denial.

And consciousness is not reducible to the material level. Thomas Huxley recognised this over a century and a half ago in his *Essays*: "There is a third thing in the universe [in addition to force and matter], to wit, consciousness, which . . . I can not see to be matter or force, or any conceivable modification of either."

Time has passed, but the irreducibility has persisted. The physicist Erich Harth explains the rock-wall of sheer incomprehensibility that blocks all attempts to reduce consciousness: "It is not just that we don't know the mechanisms that give rise to it. We have difficulty in seeing how any mechanism can give rise to it."

Given that consciousness is real and irreducible, accommodating it in our conceptions of the world will require expansion of those conceptions. The history of science reminds us forcefully that the willingness to expand our conceptions is the engine of progress.

In the nineteenth century, science seemed stalled by its inability to account for electromagnetism in terms of mechanical forces. Only when electromagnetism was recognised as a fundamental force in nature did science continue its onward journey. Today, the arena of consciousness studies similarly beckons science to expand its frontiers.

REDIRECTING THE QUEST

If science decides to explore this opportunity, the Vedic literatures of ancient India can serve as a veritable gold mine. Vedic wisdom has always been consciousness-conscious. It has an extensive body of knowledge that analyses consciousness and a potent repository of techniques with which to experiment with consciousness.

The *Bhagavad-gita* (2.17) states that consciousness is the energy of a non-material or spiritual particle: the soul. After thus confirming the irreducibility of consciousness the *Gita* (13.27) outlines a two-level reality that comprises and integrates matter and spirit into a dynamic interacting whole.

For elucidating this interaction, the *Gita* (18.61) uses the metaphor of a machine: the soul uses the body as a machine (*yantra*) for functioning at the material level. So, the idea of a machine working in tandem with consciousness is found in the *Gita* written thousands of years ago. But the *Gita* doesn't assume that consciousness originates from the bodily machine—it posits consciousness as an independent reality and gives us tools for exploring this non-material reality.

Vedic wisdom is permeated with a bold ambitiousness to investigate consciousness. At the same time, it cautions against letting narrow materialism unnecessarily monopolise this research. We need to put first things first—begin with that which is known to be real. What is actually grounded in empirical reality is the factuality of our own consciousness.

Therefore, if consciousness research is not to be sabotaged by a shaky foundation, it needs to focus on what is factual instead of what is fantastical. Instead of asking, "Can machines be conscious?" it needs to ask, "Who is it that asks the question: can machines be conscious? Who is it that has the consciousness to analyse whether machines are conscious? Who is it that is evaluating this article about the possibility of machine consciousness?"

Obsession with machine consciousness—instead of consciousness *per se*—exposes an *a priori* monopolisation of consciousness research by materialism. Such materialist prejudice runs wholly counter to the spirit of open-minded enquiry that is the celebrated hallmark of science. Worse still, this partisanship sabotages the possibility of scientific research getting to the heart of consciousness because the material level can reach only to the shadows of consciousness at best.

If science can successfully resist materialist imperialism, then Vedic wisdom opens for it avenues to study consciousness in its purity and originality: consciousness disentangled from matter, consciousness ranging free.

Instead of the materialist fixation with studying consciousness second-hand by struggling to incarnate it in a machine Vedic wisdom offers a refreshing alternative: study consciousness first-hand by dis-incarnating it from the physical body.

For this first-hand study of consciousness, Vedic wisdom provides time-honoured practices collectively known as yoga. These practices progressively lead the consciousness researcher to a state of limpid inner perception known as *samadhi*. In that state, the *Gita* (6.20-23) indicates, one can perceive consciousness in its reality, beauty, and glory. That perception of pristine consciousness is far more illuminating than the phantasmagoria of machine consciousness.

Why should consciousness research settle for anything less than the real thing?

APPENDIX THREE

❦

GHOSTS
DEMYSTIFIED

Do ghosts exist?

Yes would be the answer of many people across history and geography. Nearly universal in human experience are reports of people seeing, hearing, or perceiving disembodied ghostly beings that seem to act in mysterious and frightening ways. In our scientific times, many of us may tend to dismiss the whole idea of ghosts as unscientific folk fantasy. However, several eminent scientists have taken ghosts quite seriously.

Prominent among these ghost-believing scientists is the English naturalist scientist Alfred Wallace, who was the co-founder of the theory of evolution.

In his autobiography *My Life: A Record of Events and Opinions*, he outlines how the evidence forced him to give up his anti-ghost bias: "The majority of people today have been brought up in the belief that miracles, ghosts, and the whole series of strange phenomena here described cannot exist; that they are contrary to the laws of nature; that they are the superstitions of a bygone age; and that therefore they are necessarily either impostures or delusions. There is no place in the fabric of their thought into which such facts can be fitted. When I first began this inquiry it was the same with myself. The facts did not fit into my then existing fabric of thought. All my preconceptions, all my knowledge, all my belief in the supremacy of science and of natural law were against the possibility of such phenomena. And even when, one by one, the facts were forced upon me without possibility of escape from them, still . . . 'spirit was the last thing I could give in to.' Every other possible solution was tried and rejected . . . We ask our readers not for belief, but for doubt of their own infallibility on this question; we ask for inquiry and patient experiment before hastily concluding that we are, all of us, mere dupes and idiots as regards a subject to which we have devoted our best mental faculties and powers of observation for many years."

Another eminent scientist who was convinced by the evidence was the reputed American psychologist William James: "So when I turn to the rest of the evidence, ghosts and all, I cannot carry with me the irreversibly negative bias of the 'rigorously scientific' mind, with its presumption as to what the true order of nature ought to be." (*William James on Psychical Research* by Gardner and Ballou Murphy)

Since the observations by these researchers, the weight of the evidence has only increased as many well-documented books report evidence accumulated using rigorous scientific procedures by several paranormal researchers.

Paralleling this significant evidence and possibly boosted by it is the substantial public belief in the existence of ghosts. A Gallup survey conducted in 1990 showed that:

- 29 percent Americans believed in ghosts haunting houses
- 1 in 10 Americans claim to have seen or been in the presence of a ghost

Despite this increasing documented evidence and popular acceptance, the concept of ghosts remains unacceptable for most scientists. A primary reason for this is that modern materialist science has no conceptual structure within which to account for the existence of ghosts.

But this limitation is not intrinsic to science *per se*, though it may be essential to materialist science. Significantly however, there is no scientific reason to assume that all science has to be materialist because there is no scientific evidence that all of reality exists only at the material level.

For those who are open-minded and adventurous enough to explore non-materialist worldviews Vedic wisdom offers a systematic explanatory framework for understanding the existence of ghosts.

THREE LEVELS OF BEING

To aid our understanding of ghosts, let's revisit the three levels of existence discussed earlier: the gross material level, the subtle material level, and the spiritual level.

Germane to our discussion of ghosts is the difference between the mind and the soul. The mind though invisible is not spiritual; it is material, though made of a subtle material substance that renders it invisible to our gross senses. The mind being material is not conscious; the soul alone is conscious. The mind belongs to the subtle level that is intermediate between the spiritual level on one side and the gross material level on the other side. From this intermediate position, the mind acts as the conduit for the consciousness of the soul to interact with the gross body. Functionally, the mind becomes a storehouse of impressions acquired from interacting with the gross material level. These impressions comprise, among other things, memories of the past and desires for the future.

With this grounding in basic Vedic ontology, let's now understand how and why some people become ghosts.

THE DISEMBODIED AND DISTRESSED

At the time of death, the soul, accompanied by the subtle body, leaves the gross body. Normally, the soul gets a new gross body according to its karma. But in exceptional cases when the soul does not get a next gross body, then it stays in a disembodied state. Souls living this disembodied existence are called ghosts.

Of course, ghosts are not entirely disembodied; they still have a subtle body. But in general parlance, the word *body* connotes a gross body; so the state of existence without that body is called *disembodied*.

Why don't these ghosts get a physical body?

1. **Suicide**: Some people destroy their physical body through suicide prematurely, that is, before they have become entitled by their karmic destiny to receive a new body. Due to such unnatural self-destruction, they sentence themselves to a disembodied existence as ghosts till they are allocated a new physical body. Thus, frustrated people who imagine that death is the end of existence and so commit suicide to become free

from misery find themselves in an even more miserable existence as a ghost.

2. **Extreme attachment**: Those who die with extreme attachment to their physical body, environment, or possessions, may also become ghosts. During such deaths, the excessive and intensive obsession of the mind with the past may prevent the soul from moving on to a next body, thereby keeping it disembodied.

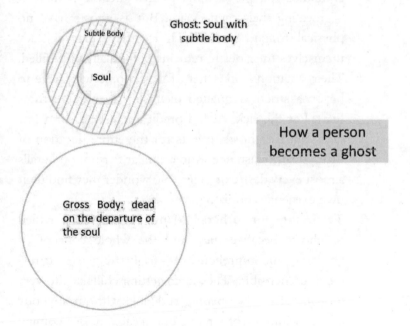

Ghost: Soul with subtle body

Subtle Body

Soul

How a person becomes a ghost

Gross Body: dead on the departure of the soul

FRUSTRATING AND TERRIFYING PREDICAMENT

The anomalous disembodied condition of the ghosts is agonising for them and terrifying for others. Let's see why:

1. **Agonising for ghosts:** Ghosts have a mind just like all of us. Their mind, like ours is filled with memories and desires developed from their indulgences in their past embodied existences. But they, unlike us have no gross body with which to satisfy those desires. Thus, for example, their memories may stimulate their desire for a favourite delicacy. And as the subtle body contains subtle senses they may even perceive others— embodied people—enjoying that delicacy, thereby aggravating their own desire. But as ghosts have no physical tongue with which to enjoy that delicacy themselves their desire remains perpetually unfulfilled. Their situation is like that of sick people who have to be on a strictly regulated diet while watching others feast. For the sick, such a predicament lasts for a few days. But for ghosts, it lasts for the entire duration of their ghostly existence. And a similar frustration befalls almost every desire of theirs. No wonder they find their own existence agonizing.

2. **Terrifying for others:** Many people are terrified of ghosts because they find the whole concept of ghosts incomprehensible—frighteningly, eerily, incomprehensible. They start getting chills at the very thought of doors opening suddenly without anybody in the vicinity or of strange untraceable noises coming from some area. Few things turn off prospective house buyers as much as the rumour, be it true or false, that the house is haunted.

For most people, the possibility of encountering a ghost is scary enough, but the prospect of being possessed by one is bloodcurdling. Possession refers to the disconcerting phenomenon in which a ghost enters into the gross body of a person, takes control of that gross body and uses it as an instrument for fulfilling its own desires. The person, thus possessed, often speaks and acts in ways that differ markedly from their normal ways of speech and behaviour.

During the period of possession, the possessed person exhibits a personality different from their normal personality because that normal personality has been suppressed by the ghost's personality. This alteration of personality frequently perplexes and perturbs the possessed person's relatives. Anecdotal accounts of such possessions escalate the fear of ghosts in the minds of the general public.

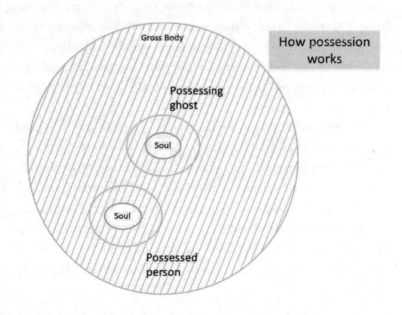

EVAPORATING THE HAZE OF EERINESS

Vedic wisdom can evaporate this haze of eeriness surrounding ghosts. It demystifies the nature of ghostly existence and helps us see ghosts not so much as *malevolent* beings but as *miserable* beings. Of course, some ghosts may be malevolent, especially towards people who have wronged them in their past embodied existence. But in general, ghosts are primarily miserable because of the unfulfillable cravings endemic to their disembodied existence. The pressure of these frustrations often turns them towards violence and sometimes malevolence.

The Vedic triadic vision of reality—gross matter, subtle matter, and spirit—helps us make sense of the mysterious-seeming behaviours of ghost that defy the laws of materialist science. These laws have been postulated primarily by observing and analysing the behaviour of gross matter. As the mind is a subtle material element, not a gross one, its actions are not limited by these laws of materialist science. No wonder then that ghosts existing as they do on the mental plane, can act in ways that baffle and unnerve people who have been taught to believe that everything in nature follows the laws of materialist science.

The uncanny power of ghosts is indicated in the *Bhagavata Purana* (5.5.21-22), which places ghosts above humans in the universal hierarchy of living beings: "Superior to human beings are ghosts because they have no material bodies." The Vedic texts explain that ghosts thrive in conditions of ignorance and illusion. So those people who habitually keep themselves in such conditions by, say, intoxication are more likely to have a weakened mind more vulnerable to attacks by ghosts.

We can make ourselves largely invulnerable to such incorporeal attacks by adopting an enlightening mode of living, centred on regulating worldly indulgence and seeking realisation of life's higher realities. Vedic wisdom recommends such a mode of living primarily for furthering our spiritual growth, which is life's foremost goal. Nonetheless, such a mode of living that steers clear of self-defeating indulgences offers the fringe benefit of protection from attacks by ghostly creatures.

For dealing with attacks by ghosts, Vedic wisdom equips us with not only preventive but also curative insights. Devotional activities like collective recitation of sacred mantras as in *kirtans*, can exorcise both places that are haunted, and people who are possessed.

GOING BEYOND ALL MISERIES

Significantly, though Vedic wisdom acknowledges the existence of ghosts, it doesn't uncritically place the blame for all strange-seeming behaviour on them. Despite explaining the existence of ghosts and declaring the exorcising potency of the holy name, Vedic wisdom doesn't give much importance to either. It asserts that human life is meant for a far more important purpose than preoccupation with ghosts, be it in the form of a morbid fascination, a paranoid fear, or a dogmatic denial.

Disciplining the mind by fixing it on God is the most effective way to deal with all the problems of material existence—becoming ghosts ourselves, or being haunted by ghosts, or being tormented by the troubles of the mind that some might ascribe to ghosts, or all other problems that are ultimately the karmic reactions for misdeeds impelled by the uncontrolled mind.

Human life holds the glorious potential of granting us immortality if we use it to redirect our love from the ephemeral to the eternal, from matter to God. Restoring to us our lost right to immorality as spiritual beings is the ultimate treasure of Vedic wisdom. The explanatory expertise of Vedic wisdom in accounting coherently for phenomena like ghosts—phenomena that baffle materialist science and compel it to live in perpetual denial—can serve as a faith-booster for us as we explore its higher spiritual insights and relish its devotional gifts.

BIBLIOGRAPHY

A. C. Bhaktivedanta Swami Prabhupāda. *Bhagavad-gita as it is*. Mumbai: Bhaktivedanta Book Trust, 2011.

A. C. Bhaktivedanta Swami Prabhupāda. *Coming back: the science of reincarnation : based on the teachings of his Divine Grace A.C. Bhaktivedanta Swami Prabhupāda*. Los Angeles Calif: Bhaktivedanta Book Trust, 1984.

A. C. Bhaktivedanta Swami Prabhupāda. *Consciousness: the missing link: scientists of the Bhaktivedanta Institute examine key underlying concepts of the modern life sciences in light of India's age-old Vedic knowledge*. Los Angeles: Bhaktivedanta Book Trust, 1980.

A. C. Bhaktivedanta Swami Prabhupāda, *Srimad Bhagavatam*. Los Angeles: Bhaktivedanta Book Trust, 1985.

Atkinson, William Walker. *Reincarnation and the law of Karma the old-new world-doctrine of rebirth and spiritual cause and effect*. Waiheke Island: Floating Press, 2009. http://public.eblib. com/choice/publicfullrecord.aspx?p=435849.

Baars, Bernard, William P. Banks, and James B. Newman. *Essential Sources In The Scientific Study Of Consciousness*. Cambridge, Mass: MIT Press, 2003. http://search.ebscohost. com/login.aspx?direct=true&scope=site&db=nlebk&db=nla bk&AN=100034.

Barbour, Ian G. *When science meets religion*. San Francisco: Harper, SanFrancisco, 2000.

Barr, Stephen M. *Modern physics and ancient faith*. Notre Dame, Ind: University of Notre Dame Press, 2003.

Berlinski, Berlinski. *The Devil's delusion: Atheism and its scientific pretensions*. New York: Crown Forum, 2008.

Beauregard, Mario, and Denyse O'Leary. *The spiritual brain: A neuroscientist's case for the existence of the soul.* New York: HarperOne, 2007.

Bowman, Carol. *Children's past lives: How past life memories affect your child.* New York: Bantam Books, 1997.

Bowman, Carol. *Children's past lives: How past life experiences can affect your child.* Shaftesbury: Element, 1997.

Bowman, Carol. *Return from heaven: Beloved relatives reincarnated within your family.* New York: HarperCollins, 2001.

Brooks, Michael. *13 Things That Don't Make Sense: The Most Intriguing Scientific Mysteries of Our Time.* London: Profile, 2010.

Brown, Stephen F. and Khaled Anatolios. *Catholicism & Orthodox Christianity.* New York: Facts on File, 2002.

Brown, Stephen F. *Protestantism.* New York: Facts on File, 2002.

Chalmers, David John. *The character of consciousness.* Oxford: Oxford University Press, 2010.

Chalmers, David John. *The Conscious Mind: In Search of a Fundamental Theory.* New York: Oxford University Press, 1996. http://site.ebrary.com/id/10279015

Cooper, Irving S. *Reincarnation, A Hope of the World.* Wheaton, Ill: Theosophical Pub. House, 1979.

Cremo, Michael A. *Human devolution: A Vedic Alternative to Darwin's Theory.* Los Angeles, CA: Bhaktivedanta Book Pub., 2003.

Devamrita. *Searching for Vedic India.* Los Angeles: Bhaktivedanta Book Trust, 2002.

DeWitt, Richard. *Worldviews: An Introduction to The History and Philosophy of Science.* Malden, MA: Blackwell Pub., 2004.

Doidge, Norman. *The brain that changes itself: Stories of Personal

Triumph from the Frontiers of Brain Science. New York: Viking, 2007.

Freeman, Anthony. *Consciousness a guide to the debates.* Santa Barbara, Calif: ABC-CLIO, 2003. http://ebooks.abc-clio.com/?isbn=9781576077924.

Gordon, Matthew. *Islam.* New York, NY: Facts on File, 1991.

Géley, Gustave, and Stanley De Brath. *From the Unconscious to the Conscious.* New York: Harper & Brothers, 1921.

Hall, Manly P. *Reincarnation: The Cycle of Necessity.* Los Angeles: Philosophical Research Society, 1967.

Haught, John F. *Science and religion: From Conflict to Conversation.* New York: Paulist Press, 1995.

Haraldsson, Erlendur, and Majd Abu-Izzeddin. *Development of Certainty about the Correct Deceased Person in a Case of the Reincarnation Type in Lebanon: The Case of Nazih Al-Danaf.* Journal of Scientific Exploration, 2002, Vol. 16, No.3, pp. 363-380.

Head, Joseph, and S. L. Cranston. *Reincarnation: An East-West Anthology.* New York: Julian Press, 1961.

Head, Joseph, and S. L. Cranston. *Reincarnation In World Thought; A Living Study of Reincarnation In All Ages; Including Selections From The World's Religions, Philosophies, Sciences, And Great Thinkers Of The Past And Present.* New York: Julian Press, 1967.

Heisenberg, Werner. *Physics and philosophy: The Revolution in Modern Science.* New York: Harper, 1958.

Herbert, Nick. *Quantum reality: Beyond the New Physics.* Garden City, N.Y.: Anchor Press/Doubleday, 1985.

Huxley, Thomas Henry, and William Jay Youmans. *The Elements of Physiology and Hygiene; a Text-Book for Educational Institutions.* New York: D. Appleton, 1873.

Kandel, Eric R. *In Search of Memory: The Emergence of a New Science of Mind.* New York: W.W. Norton & Co, 2006.

Kelly, Edward F. *Irreducible mind: Toward a Psychology for the 21st Century.* Lanham, Md: Rowman & Littlefield, 2007.

Koperski, Jeffrey. *The physics of theism: God, Physics, and the Philosophy of Science.* Chichester, West Sussex, U.K.: Wiley-Blackwell, 2015. http://site.ebrary.com/id/10986640.

Kuhn, Thomas S. *The Structure of Scientific Revolutions.* Chicago: University of Chicago Press, 1970.

Küng, Hans. *Eternal life? Life After Death As a Medical, Philosophical, and Theological Problem.* Garden City, N. Y.: Doubleday, 1984.

Leininger, Bruce, Andrea Leininger, and Ken Gross. *Soul Survivor: The Reincarnation of a World War II Fighter Pilot.* New York: Grand Central Pub., 2009.

Lewin, Roger. *Is Your Brain Really Necessary?* Science, New Series, Vol. 210, No. 4475 (Dec. 12, 1980), pp. 1232-1234 URL:http://www.jstor.org/stable/1684473

Lexon, James. *Reincarnation: Life After Death Explained.* South Carolina: CreateSpace Independent Publishing, 2012.

Lommel, Pim van. *Consciousness beyond life: The science of the near-death experience.* New York: HarperOne, 2010.

Lönnerstrand, Sture. *I have lived before: The true story of the reincarnation of Shanti Devi.* Huntsville, AR: Ozark Mountain Publishers, 1998.

MacGregor, Geddes. *Reincarnation in Christianity: A new vision of the role of rebirth in Christian thought.* Wheaton, Ill: Theosophical Pub. House, 1978.

Martin, Stephen Hawley. *Reincarnation: Good News for Open-*

Minded Christians & Other Truth-Seekers. Florida: The Oaklea Press, 2015.

Martin, Barbara Y., and Dimitri Moraitis. *Karma and reincarnation: unlocking your 800 lives to enlightenment*. New York: Jeremy P. Tarcher/Penguin, 2010.

McClelland, Norman C. *Encyclopedia of Reincarnation and Karma*. Jefferson, N.C.: McFarland, 2010. http://site.ebrary.com/id/10375836.

Mills, Antonia. *Inferences from the Case of Ajendra Singh Chauhan: The Effect of Parental Questioning, of Meeting the "Previous Life" Family, an Aborted Attempt to Quantify Probabilities, and the Impact on His Life as a Young Adult*. Journal of Scientific Exploration (2004) Vol. 18, No. 4, 609–641.

Mills, Antonia. *Moslem Cases of the Reincarnation Type in Northern India: A Test of the Hypothesis of Imposed Identification Part I: Analysis of 26 Cases*. Journal of Scientific Exploration (1990) Vol. 4, No. 2, pp. 171-188.

Miller, Greg. *What Is the Biological Basis of Consciousness?* Washington D. C.: Science, 2005. http://science.sciencemag.org/content/309/5731/79.full

Nagel, Thomas. *Mind and Cosmos: Why the Materialist Neo-Darwinian Conception of Nature is Almost Certainly False*. New York: Oxford University Press, 2012.

Nayak, G. C. *Evil and the retributive hypothesis*. India: Motilal Banarsidass Publishers, 1993.

Newton, Michael. *Journey of souls: Case studies of life between lives*. St. Paul, Minn: Llewellyn, 1994.

Nissanka, H. S. S. *The girl who was reborn: A Case Study Suggestive of Reincarnation*. Colombo: S. Godage Brothers, 2001.

Olivelle, Patrick. *The early Upanisads annotated text and translation*. New York: Oxford University Press, 1998. http://site.ebrary.com/id/10278193.

Olivelle, Patrick. *Saṃnyāsa Upaniṣads: Hindu Scriptures on Asceticism and Renunciation*. New York: Oxford University Press, 1992. http://www.dawsonera.com/depp/reader/protected/external/AbstractView/S9780195361377.

Okasha, Samir. *Philosophy of science: A Very Short Introduction*. Oxford: Oxford University Press, 2002.

Papineau, David, and Howard Selina. *Introducing consciousness: A Graphic Guide*. London: Icon., 2010.

Parnia, Sam. *What happens when we die: A Groundbreaking Study into the Nature of Life and Death*. Carlsbad, Calif: Hay House, 2006.

Peat, F. David. *From certainty to uncertainty: The story of science and ideas in the twentieth century*. Washington, D.C.: Joseph Henry Press, 2002. http://site.ebrary.com/id/10039741.

Penfield, Wilder. *The mystery of the mind: A Critical Study of Consciousness and The Human Brain*. Princeton, N.J.: Princeton University Press, 1975.

Prophet, Elizabeth Clare, and Erin L. Prophet. *Reincarnation: The Missing Link In Christianity*. Corwin Springs, MT: Summit University Press, 1997.

Radin, Dean I. *The conscious universe: The scientific truth of psychic phenomena*. New York, N.Y.: HarperEdge, 1997.

Ring, Kenneth, and Sharon Cooper. *Mindsight: Near-death and Out-Of-Body Experiences In The Blind*. Palo Alto, Calif: William James Center for Consciousness Studies, 1999.

Rosen, Steven. *Essential Hinduism*. Westport, Conn: Praeger, 2006.

Rosen, Steven. *The reincarnation controversy: Uncovering the Truth in the World Religions.* Badger, CA: Torchlight Pub., 1997.

Sabom, Michael B. *Light & death: One doctor's fascinating account of near-death experiences.* Grand Rapids, Mich: Zondervan, 1998.

Sabom, Michael B. *Recollections of death: A medical investigation.* New York: Harper & Row, 1982.

Sargeant, Winthrop, and Christopher Key Chapple. *The Bhagavad Gita.* Albany, N.Y.: State University of New York Press, 2009. http://site.ebrary.com/id/10573935

Schwartz, Jeffrey, and Sharon Begley. *The mind and the brain: Neuroplasticity and the power of mental force.* New York: Regan Books/HarperCollins Publ., 2002.

Series Edited by O'Brien, Joanne, and Martin Palmer. *Hinduism, Fourth Edition.* Chelsea House, 2009. http://www.myilibrary.com?id=243495

Shroder, Tom. *Old souls: scientific search for proof of past lives.* London: Simon & Schuster, 1999.

Singh, Nikky-Guninder Kaur. *Sikhism.* New York: Facts on File, 1993.

Smith, Huston. *Beyond the postmodern mind: The place of meaning in a global civilization.* Wheaton, Ill: Quest Books, 2003.

Smith, Huston. *Forgotten truth: The common vision of the world's religions.* San Francisco: Harper San Francisco, 1992.

Smith, Huston. *The World's Religions: Our Great Wisdom Traditions.* San Francisco: Harper San Francisco, 1991.

Smith, Huston. *Why religion matters: The Fate of The Human Spirit In An Age of Disbelief.* New York, N.Y.: HarperCollins, 2001.

Stapp, Henry P. *A report on the Gaudiya Vaishnava Vedanta Form of Vedic Ontology.* Bombay, India: Bhaktivedanta Institute, 1994.

Stemman, Roy. *The big book of reincarnation examining the evidence that we have all lived before.* San Antonio, Texas: Hierophant Pub., 2012. http://search.ebscohost.com/login.aspx?direct=true&scope=site&db=nlebk&db=nlabk&AN=494445.

Stevenson, Ian. *Cases of the reincarnation type.* Charlottesville: University Press of Virginia, 1975.

Stevenson, Ian. *European cases of the reincarnation type.* Jefferson, N.C.: McFarland & Co., Publishers, 2003.

Stevenson, Ian. *Reincarnation and biology: A contribution to the etiology of birthmarks and birth defects.* Westport, Conn: Praeger, 1997.

Stevenson, Ian. *Twenty cases suggestive of reincarnation.* Charlottesville: University Press of Virginia, 1974.

Stevenson, Ian. *Where reincarnation and biology intersect.* Westport, Conn: Praeger, 1997.

Tarnas, Richard. *The passion of the Western mind: Understanding the ideas that have shaped our world view.* New York: Harmony Books, 1991.

Thompson, Richard L., *Alien identities: Ancient insights into modern UFO phenomena.* San Diego: Govardhan Hill Pub., 1993.

Thompson, Richard L. *God & science: Divine causation and the laws of natures.* Alachua, Fla: Govardhan Hill Pub., 2004.

Thompson, Richard L. *Maya: The world as virtual reality.* Alachua, Fla: Govardhan Hill Pub., 2003.

Thompson, Richard L. *Mechanistic and nonmechanistic science: An investigation into the nature of consciousness and form.* Lynbrook, N.Y.: Bala Books, 1981.

Thompson, Richard F., and Stephen A. Madigan. *Memory: The key to consciousness.* Washington, D.C.: Joseph Henry Press, 2005.

Tichenor, Henry M. *Theory of reincarnation.* Girard, Kan: Haldeman-Julius Co., 1924.

Tucker, Jim B. *Life before life: A scientific investigation of children's memories of previous lives.* New York: St. Martin's Press, 2005.

Tucker, Jim B. *Return to life: Extraordinary cases of children who remember past lives.* New York: St. Martin's Press, 2013.

Walker, E. D. *Reincarnation: a study of forgotten truth.* New Hyde Park, N.Y. : University Books, 1965.

Wangu, Madhu Bazaz. *Buddhism: World religions.* New York, N.Y.: Facts on File, 1992.

Weiss, Brian L. *Many lives, many masters: The true story of a prominent psychiatrist, his young patient and the past-life therapy that changed both of their lives.* London: Piatkus, 1994.

Weiss, Brian L. *Through time into healing.* New York: Simon & Schuster, 1992.

Whitton, Joel L., and Joe Fisher. *Life between life: Scientific explorations into the void separating one incarnation from the next.* New York, N.Y.: Warner Books, 1988.

Zarandi, Mehrdad M. *Science and the myth of progress.* Bloomington, Ind: World Wisdom, 2003.

ACKNOWLEDGEMENTS

My first thanks to my foremost spiritual guide B R Swami who asked me to research and write on this topic and who meticulously reviewed this book

Many friends helped me in researching the material for this book. Dr Siddhartha Reddy, Dr Abhishek Ghosh, Amol Katkar, Anirudha Iyer, Manish Vithlani, Varun Sharma and Sanjay Sharma.

My thanks also to my agent Kanishka Gupta and the team at Fingerprint! Publishing.

Chaitanya Charan is a mentor, life coach, and monk. Building on his engineering degree from the Government College of Engineering, Pune, he complemented his scientific training with a keen spiritual sensitivity. For over two decades, he has researched ancient wisdom-texts and practiced their teachings in a living yoga tradition.

Author of over twenty books, he writes the world's only Gita-daily feature (gitadaily.com), wherein he has penned over two thousand daily meditations on the Bhagavad-gita. Known for his systematic talks and incisive question-answer sessions, he has spoken on spiritual topics at universities and companies worldwide from Australia to America.

NOTES

NOTES